Y0-BQX-018

The Husky Hitman

Dave Hoffmann
and Derek Johnson

The Husky

Hitman

The Life and Times of a Linebacker in the Golden Age of Washington Football

OTHER BOOKS BY DEREK JOHNSON

Husky Football in the Don James Era
The Dawgs of War (Tuiasosopo's Rose Bowl Season)
Bow Down to Willingham

Derek Johnson Books

PO Box 8298
Port Orchard, WA 98366
DerekJohnsonBooks.com

© Copyright 2012 by Dave Hoffmann and Derek Johnson

All rights reserved. No part of this publication may be reproduced, stored in a retrieval system or transmitted, in any form, or by any means, electronic, recorded, photocopied, or otherwise, without prior permission of the copyright owners, except by a reviewer who may quote brief passages in a review.

Printed in the United States of America

ISBN 978-0-9793271-7-9

Edited by Dawn Cahoon
Interior design and layout by Jonathan Gullery
All photographs not otherwise credited are reproduced with permission from Doug Glant and Dave Hoffmann.
For information regarding special discounts for bulk purchases, please contact us at info@derekjohnsonbooks.com

Acknowledgments

Thanks to my former teammates... There are too many experiences and friendships to try to list them all. Because of the intense brotherhood we had, I feel I don't have to. During our era at Washington, we possessed talent, work ethic and focus, but what set us apart even more was our love for each other. To this day, I know that if I'm ever in the battle of my life, you are the warriors I want at my side... and I pray you feel the same about me.

Thanks to my brother Steve Hoffmann... Not many people ever have the joy of having your own brother in the huddle with them, but we shared that indescribable thrill. I'm forever thankful.

Thanks to chaplain and former UW linebacker, Mike Rohrbach... He was and continues to be a great friend to all of us. His support and spiritual guidance meant the world to our team. To this day, he continues to reach out to young athletes in the Seattle community through his non-profit organization, Run to Win.

Some members of our team and staff have since gone on to Heaven and we miss them all... including Travis Spring and our brother linebacker Jaime Fields. God bless their families.

Thanks to Derek Johnson... It was a joy to rehash these memories during our many discussions while making this book.

Thanks to Husky fans... You never got tired of cheering for our big hits, forced turnovers and our "3 and outs" as we ran off the field. You knew your football and appreciated hard work, preparation and of course.... GREAT DEFENSE!

Finally, thanks to my children, Callie and Jaeger... May you continue to grow and learn from both my successes and mistakes. Always follow and be thankful to the Lord. You are the pride and joy of Mom and I and we love you.

- Dave Hoffmann, August 2012

The Husky Hitman

PROLOGUE

DAVE HOFFMANN WAS FIRED UP from the phone call. With gritted teeth and a big grin, the former All-American linebacker roamed throughout his Maryland home, stalking prey. He grabbed his wife Elle and kissed her while giving her the glad news. He went looking for his two kids, 7-year old son Jaeger and 11-year old daughter Callie. He confronted them in the living room, tackling them both and dropping them to the floor, and telling them of their upcoming trip while the vigorous wrestling match ensued.

The 39-year old Hoffmann had just received word from his alma mater, the University of Washington, that they were going to honor him as a Husky Legend during the 2009 Apple Cup football game against Washington State. The Husky Legend tradition began in 2005 introducing former Husky football players to the crowd at the end of the third quarter of home games.

Having lived and worked for many years on the east coast, Dave hadn't seen a game in Seattle in almost a decade. Here was a chance to return to Husky Stadium and bring his family, showing them where some of the happiest days of his life took place. Over the years, Dave's kids had heard many Husky football stories at the dinner table. Stories about old buddies on the team and all the great things they did and the good times they had. Stories of playing for great coaches like Don James and Jim Lambright. Stories of the three Rose Bowls they played in and the National Championship they won. Stories that expressed how much their dad loved being a linebacker.

Most of all, he told them the stories of high speed destruction unleashed by the greatest defense in college football history.

"A few years back, my dad gave me old VHS tapes of my games," Hoffmann recalls. "When my daughter was young she asked me, 'Daddy, how come when you guys tackle the ball carrier you then get up and tackle each other?' That's when it really hit me that in the eyes of a kid, she could see the passion that we had for football and each other. It was so contagious. We stopped hitting the other team after the whistle, but we started jumping on each other and had a good time. We had explosive energy and emotion that couldn't be bottled up between whistles. We were excited for whoever made the play and we all wanted a piece of the celebration!

"Even today, my kids always comment about how fired up I get, and how they expect it on a daily basis. I'm a physical guy and I get jacked up. When the Huskies are playing on TV, I watch whenever possible. If they play great defense then I'm real pleased. But when they get the ball run down their throats, I get fired up—and the whole house hears about it."

The University of Washington provided Hoffmann with a parking pass — about two miles from the stadium, beneath the dorms where he and former teammate James Clifford used to live. He pulled into the parking garage and the family emerged from the car. Jaeger had a mini Hoffmann #54 jersey on. An older man standing nearby with his wife yelled over: "Now THAT guy was a player! Dave Hoffmann knew how to play the game!"

Jaeger stood there with a little grin on his face and just let the guy talk. The man expressed how much fun it was to watch Dave Hoffmann play linebacker and that those were some of the best teams in college football history. Finally, Elle chimed in. "Well, this is actually Dave Hoffmann's son." Laughter all around. It turned out the guy was a longtime Husky fan but his wife was a Washington State Cougar, so it was a mixed marriage.

The Hoffmanns walked with them for a few minutes talking and laughing about the old days. Soon, Husky Stadium loomed before them. Dating back to 1920, the stadium had been carved from the earth and currently had a capacity of 72,500. The giant cantilevered upper decks, hovering overhead, flanked the field and served as an echo chamber for crowd noise.

Before going inside, the family wandered the vast expanse of the north parking lot, which was congested with RVs and cars festooned with purple and gold, while swarms of Husky fans tailgated and socialized. Many recognized Hoffmann, and welcomed him and his family with open arms. "When you're playing, the tailgating experience is something you don't get to see," Hoffmann says. "It's what college football is all about. People sharing their food and beverages and talking and laughing and having a great time."

Still with time before kickoff, Dave and his family migrated into the organized tailgate area called The Zone. He introduced his wife and kids to former teammates he hadn't seen in years. Dave exchanged exuberant hugs and loud greetings with these men, some of whom were in great shape, while others were paunchy, wore glasses or had flecks of gray in their thinning hair. These men referred to Dave with a barrage of nicknames, including "Hoff", "Hammer", "Hitman", "Hoff Daddy" and "Fifty-Four". Everyone smiled broadly. "When you play hard and train together with all the blood, sweat and tears we expelled, the bonds last forever," Dave says.

Hoff excused himself and went to be interviewed by Softy Mahler on KJR Radio. He shared his excitement of being there and what the program meant to him. Finally, the Hoffmanns entered the stadium just prior to kickoff. For three quarters they watched as quarterback Jake Locker and the Huskies worked their way toward what would be a 30-0 victory over the Cougs. It was to be Washington's first shutout in a long time following many years of dreadful football.

As the third quarter reached its conclusion, Dave went with his wife and kids to the sideline at the corner of the end zone. It was one thing to be in the stands looking down upon the field. It was something else to walk out there and feel the cushiony field turf underfoot. To stand amid the whitewash glare of powerful overhead lights and feel the surge of adrenaline signaling that 70,000 sets of eyes would soon be upon them. A UW representative came over to make sure the family was ready to go and in the right place. Never having seen a Husky Legend introduction before, Hoffmann wasn't exactly sure how these things went down. He just followed the cues.

The loud speaker blared… "PLEASE DIRECT YOUR ATTENTION TO THE WEST END ZONE…" Moments later, Hoff stepped into the end zone and made sure his family came out with him. "I had always told them how loud Husky Stadium got and how cool it was to be out there and feeling it," he says. As the PA announcer described his career, the Hitman edged out onto the field. The crowd welcomed him with an explosive roar that grew as one moment built upon the next. "I felt that familiar bond with the fans that I had when I was playing. It was a deep down in your soul kind of feeling. As the crowd got louder, I got more jacked up. I couldn't help it—I got down into my linebacker stance and slapped at the turf repeatedly with my hands. The only thing missing was being able to use my forehead against a fullback. Those days are over, unfortunately. But that was my way of honoring the fans and showing them what it meant to me and how happy I was to be back."

Hoff pivoted and saw his kids laughing and smiling. They weren't surprised by dad's behavior; this was par for the course. Hoffmann's eyes got watery. "It was emotional and humbling to be back out there," he recalls. "As we walked off the field, my kids shouted 'This is awesome!'" He slapped them on their backs while his wife beamed. They soon returned to their seats and watched as the Husky defense preserved the shutout.

The next day the family flew back home to Maryland and returned to the daily grind. A couple months later, Dave was going through his son's schoolwork when something gave him pause. Jaeger had written a short story about them going out on the field at Husky Stadium. Recalls Dave: "In his cute little handwriting, he said, 'The fans yelled hooray for Dave Hoffmann the legend! 70,000 fans can get really loud!' It was his own little way of saying he was proud."

Callie and Jaeger had seen first-hand the home field where their dad once played linebacker. For a moment, the kids had been brought into that world. A world where teams from 1990-1992 carved out an astonishing place in Husky football history.

Looking back, Hoffmann grows reflective. "I always thrilled at expending every ounce of energy I had on the field. Going into battle and winning championships. Hitting guys so hard that my helmet would dig into my forehead, causing rivulets of blood to trickle down my face. That was a special feeling for me—tangible evidence that I was doing a good job out there... that I was bringing intensity and violence to the opponent and they were feeling it.

"I appreciate those days and more importantly the people I was blessed to be surrounded by. We truly were a band of brothers, giving all we had and backing each other on and off the field. Our accomplishments were just evidence of the love we had for each other and for the game of football."

17

CHAPTER 1

AS A LITTLE KID growing up in Garland, Texas, the sounds from the football field were a siren song to little Davey Hoffmann's ears. He'd ride his BMX bike up to the school and watch the kids play organized football. The smacking of shoulder pads and the coach's whistle caused butterflies to churn in his stomach as he stood off to the side itching to be out there.

Dave would go home and constantly pester his parents to let him play football. They kept saying they would talk about it. Finally, his dad decreed, "football is a man's game. You should be closer to puberty before you can play."

Of course, that didn't stop young Hoff from daydreaming. It was the Texas of the 1970s, and football was right up there with God and country. Actually, three things dominated Texan culture – boots, hats and football. The Dallas Cowboys were in their glory days under legendary coach Tom Landry. Their roster was chock full of icons and household names… Roger Staubach, Tony Dorsett, Randy White, Drew Pearson, Ed "Too Tall" Jones, Charlie Waters and several others. Dave obsessed over that team and wanted to be a great football player like them. He envisioned himself as a running back or wide receiver, breaking long runs and making incredible catches.

Dave also loved watching college football. The Texas Longhorns and Oklahoma Sooners were two favorites. Big rivalry games got his attention. He dreamed about one day playing in a huge game like the Cotton Bowl or Rose Bowl.

Weekends found Dave wearing the Sears version jerseys of Tony Dorsett (#33) or Roger Staubach (#12). When done watching the games on TV, he'd grab his mini football and go knock on every kid's door on the street. If no one was around, he'd return home and throw the ball off his family's shingled roof to himself. In his imaginings, when he released the ball he was Staubach in the pocket, and when the ball cascaded off the roof and back into his arms, he was Drew Pearson hauling in the big catch. Dave's reverie would be periodically snapped by his mom, who got on him about all the racket and clatter.

While waiting to become a man, Dave's role model was his dad, Paul Hoffmann. The elder Hoffmann was a Lutheran minister, which made Dave a "P.K."—a Preacher's Kid. "Dad was the toughest, nicest guy I knew and I loved being around him," says Dave. "He may have been preaching The Word, but he looked like a linebacker. He was 6'3" 230 pounds, with big arms, shoulders and neck. He actually never played football because he grew up in the Bronx just down the street from Yankee Stadium. He played lots of stickball but they didn't have many grass fields to play on. He told me that he wished he could have played and I think he would have been a great linebacker."

Every Sunday, Mrs. Hoffmann loaded up the big Chevy station wagon and Dave and his two younger brothers headed to church to listen to dad preach. "Dad made it easy to be a preacher's kid," Dave says. "He was understanding and laid back. He lived the Gospel. He didn't scream it down our necks, so that made it more appealing to me. He didn't expect us to be perfect. He expected us to always do our best, and he lived by example. When I got old enough to flip through the Bible myself I realized that Dad was imitating Jesus Christ. Like I said, dad was the toughest, nicest guy I had ever met. And I realized that Jesus was the toughest guy in the world as well as being the kindest."

In young Dave's eyes, dad had his back when it counted. One day when he was nine, Dave was walking home with a buddy when a guy in his late teens started yelling that he was going to knock the teeth out of Dave's mouth and send them home in a bag. The kid was hanging out with two or three of his friends, and it wasn't the first time he menaced kids on that street. Dave didn't say anything and whispered to his buddy to keep walking. When they got home, Dave saw his dad trimming bushes in the hot Texas sun with his shirt off. Mr. Hoffmann said, "Dave, what did that guy say to you?"

"Oh, nothing."

"Dave, I'm asking you."

Dave told him. Pastor Hoffmann put the trimmer down and walked over there. Dave and his buddy hid behind the corner of the house and watched the oncoming confrontation. Mr. Hoffmann calmly asked the teenager if he would like to keep his teeth. The teenagers backpedaled a couple of steps, before apologizing. Mr. Hoffmann returned to the yard and resumed the trimming of the bushes, never saying a word about it. The teenager never bothered Dave again. "It quietly made me smile," he recalls.

Dave's own attempts at brokering justice at a young age could be rough around the edges. One day when he was five years old, there was a neighbor kid named Eddie hanging out in the Hoffmann's backyard. Dave's little brother Stevie was riding his Big Wheel around in countless zany circles. Eddie kept shouting that he wanted to ride it. Stevie kept telling him no. Little Davey was off to the side, watching closely. *"Don't even think about it,"* he thought to himself. Sure enough, Eddie surged forward and threw little Steve off the toy, before jumping aboard and maniacally peddling away. Dave charged after him and tackled Eddie, knocking him to the ground. Dave jumped to his feet and gave the kid a swift kick to the teeth, knocking out several. Eddie ran home sobbing while Stevie and Davey retreated inside. Mrs. Hoffmann, however, had heard all the commotion.

"Dave, what happened?"

"Nothing."

"I heard Eddie screaming. Is he hurt?"

"Uhh, maybe..."

"Dave, you need to go over there and apologize."

That was the last thing he wanted to do. Nevertheless, little Davey

Hoffmann walked over there and knocked on the door. "Eddie had three big sisters that were teenagers," he recalls. "But to me they seemed like grown women who were all scowling at me like I was such a bad guy. Eddie was sucking on a blood-soaked towel while his mom rubbed his head."

Dave told him, "Sorry Eddie."

His mom asked Dave, "Don't you feel better?"

"Yes ma'am," he said, before high-tailing it out of there.

When puberty finally hit, testosterone began pumping through Dave Hoffmann's system. He'd be walking down the hallways at O' Bannion Middle School and constantly think about hitting guys and knocking people over. "God was preparing my mind and body to go about playing football the way it was meant to be played. That's what dad was talking about!", he says.

When Mom and Dad gave him the green light, he knew he had enough raw talent to play for O'Bannion. The PE coaches were picking out the guys who would play for the team. They would have the kids work out and lift weights, teaching proper technique. They would have them do 7-on-7 drills. The whole setting provided good camaraderie and discipline. "When the coaches called on you, we all responded with 'yes sir' and 'no sir'", says Dave. "For kids that age it was a good thing. I didn't have a problem with that and I didn't have a problem with hard work."

When they handed Hoffmann his first uniform, they sent him and the others to the corner of the locker room to get dressed. Dave could not figure out the different places where the thigh pads, knee pads and tailbone pads were supposed to go. He watched the other guys in order to figure it out. He was nervous about going out there with pads in the wrong places. But he got it sorted out.

When out on the practice field, the coaches lined them up for one-on-one blocking drills. The intense heat of a Texas summer sun emanated from everywhere. The heat infiltrated every nook and cranny of the terrain, scorching the grass field so ragged that it resembled a Brillo pad. The kids were arranged to go against others of similar size, to see what everybody had in terms of talent. "I was fired up and ready to go," recalls Dave. "I just knew that putting my forehead through somebody and snapping my hips was really going to make the guy feel it."

Finally it was Dave's turn. He lined up in a three-point stance . The coach yelled "HIKE!" and Hoffmann launched himself forward and struck the guy across from him. The impact sent the other kid staggering backward and yelling the Lord's name in vain, before he collapsed in a heap upon the lifeless field. "That was a great feeling I had in my gut right there," says Dave. "I was like 'Man! This is a good time!'"

Hoffmann felt a big hand slap him on the back. He turned around and the coach with the push broom moustache smiled broadly with a lip full of Copenhagen. He glanced at the masking tape label on the front of Dave's helmet and said, "Hoffmann! We're going to find a place for you out here!"

"I was jacked up," Dave recalls. "I never doubted myself, but it was great to succeed like that straight out of the shoot. From then on, every chance I got on the football field, I was going to strike people with every ounce of strength I had."

Deep down inside, young Hoff knew he had the potential to be a great player. On many nights he went to sleep excited about the future. Excited about the hard work it would take to get there. Each day he was bouncing off the walls with enthusiasm to get back out onto the football field.

When Dave was younger, he believed the best part of football was catching touchdown passes and running for long gains like Tony Dorsett. But at O' Bannion, he was playing both offensive tackle and defensive end. "I cherished looking into a guy's facemask and battling one-on-one in the trenches all game long," he says.

Back in those days, there used to be uproars over schools holding guys back for a physical advantage in football games. One day, O' Bannion played a middle school from Mesquite, Texas. Dave got into his stance for the game's first play, and the guy across from him had a full blown moustache! "Not peach fuzz, but a full blown man-stache," Dave says. "I remember thinking the guy probably drove his pickup truck to the game, but after a moment of recoiling, I thought, 'Alright, let's get it on.' And we had a great battle that night."

O' Bannion made the city championship game that year. Prior to the finale, the coaches began making changes to the defense. Because Dave was the fastest player on the team, they asked him if he would like to play linebacker for the final game.

"I had been having urges to play linebacker, so those were the words I longed to hear," Dave says. "I had a great game. Nobody taught me how to read. I just went on pure instincts on running, playing and hitting. There was plenty of contact and violence in the middle there. We lost 7-0, but I was sky high afterward. After that, whenever I walked around, I told people I was a linebacker."

From that point on, Dave threw everything he had into being the best linebacker on earth. He asked his parents about getting a weight training set for their home. "We didn't have much money for luxuries and I would understand if we couldn't have swung it," recalls Dave. "But that Christmas, underneath blankets in the living room, was a weight set my dad assembled for me. I looked at him with astonishment."

Usually in the Hoffmann home, if someone wanted something expensive it was considered special and to be earned by the sweat of the brow. Dave had something special in mind. He mowed lawns and worked paper routes to save money.

"Dave saved up his money and got a great boom box," recalls his younger brother Steve. "He was a big hit in the neighborhood. He had a Mongoose BMX bike and I had one too. We had big old baskets on the front. We delivered the *Garland Daily News*. It was a small paper but we had one hundred subscriptions to deliver on the afternoons or very early on the weekends. It taught us independence and how to earn money and make good decisions. Dave loved to play that boom box while he worked out."

Dave taped songs off the radio that would get him fired up. He'd go into the garage and close all the doors and blast that music while training with fanatical intensity. The neighbors would hear the racket and shake their heads at that maniac Hoffmann kid. But for Dave, it felt good to have that much aggression and passion to get into this football thing. By that point in his life, his mind was squarely on defense. The way he now saw it, the world was comprised of hunters and gatherers. Guys on defense were the hunters, the aggressors, the Gladiators. Guys on offense, with some exceptions, were gatherers, looking at the game through a different lens.

At some point Dave would be called into the house for dinner. Sweating, bouncing off the walls, jabbering nonstop, family members couldn't always understand what he was saying. The kid had a motor, and on many evenings his fuel tank seemed inexhaustible. He would seek out his brothers and accost them for wrestling matches. When the boys got too loud or Mrs. Hoffmann feared for her furniture's survival, she'd yell out "HEY, COOL YOUR JETS!" The boys knew to take it outside. Amid the fresh air, they'd play sports or wrestle some more until the streetlights came on, after which they'd straggle back home. As he got ready for bed, Hoff would hear his mom's voice ring out across the house, "Good night, Dave."

Life was going great, but things were about to change. In the Lutheran church, there's what is called a Call. It's when they give a pastor an offer to preach elsewhere. Paul Hoffmann received a call from Holy Cross Lutheran Church in Los Gatos, California. He went out there to check it out and came back home to Texas. Dave almost didn't want to know what he was thinking. Nothing was said for a few days. One day, young Hoff rode his BMX bike down to a pond with his fishing pole and some bait to catch some catfish. When he got back home, his mom approached and acted extra, extra nice. Normally she would tell her boys that if they wanted lunch to grab something from the fridge. But this time she said, "Dave, would you like me to make you some lunch?" Hoff said sure, but knew something was up. She sweetly made him a tuna fish sandwich as Dave waited for the other boot to drop.

Dad broke the news that the family was moving to the Bay Area—San Jose, California. Dave started crying. He shouted, "Tell them you're not coming!" But the decision was final. Davey went outside, still crying, and rode his bike back down to the same pond. He hung out for awhile, skipping rocks across the water's surface, and let the news soak in. Finally, he decided to accept it like a man and headed back home. He had faith in his dad and knew he wouldn't make a rash decision without a lot of thought and prayer.

When he walked back through the front door he was done with crying. Dave Hoffmann knew it would be tough saying goodbye to his friends, but he also had faith that things would be okay.

CHAPTER 2

WHEN THE HOFFMANNS ARRIVED in San Jose in December 1983, the transition for Dave was generally positive. He enrolled at John Muir Middle School, and immediately became known as the new kid with different clothes who talked funny. He had a strong Texas accent, and all the kids called him "Tex". There were always popular kids at school but he wasn't one of them. "I never had the trendy clothes or fanciest things," says Dave. "But I always had what I needed."

Mr. Hoffmann knew Dave loved basketball, and suggested that he try to get onto the school's team. They had already started their season and were 8-0. The coach told Dave to meet him after school out back on the asphalt court with the chain nets. Dave worked out for him and performed well. The coach then asked him to reach up and touch the backboard; Dave leaped and grabbed the rim. The coach's eyes got as big as saucers. Just like the football coach back in Texas, the coach said, "Hoffmann, we're going to find a place for you!" Dave had found a home. The team went 26-1 and Hoffmann was voted all-league.

Come the fall of 1984, Dave began attending Pioneer High School. His main challenge growing up was a stuttering problem. His mom had always been telling him that he talked too fast. She said he needed to slow down or she would send him to a speech therapist. "I had a motor," Dave says. "If you overheard me yapping you would think, 'Man, that guy is going to town!' But my stuttering problem came mostly from trying to get the first word out. Especially when reading something. Once I get going, I'm okay, because I've always been a good reader and a quick thinker. But getting the first word out could be trouble. Even today, I still have occasional problems. I will try to leave someone a phone message and the machine will go dead on me before I get the first word out. I simply hang up and try again. It never happens with informal calls to friends, but it does happen periodically. As far as I know, there's no rhyme or reason for it. I've never had trouble getting up before a group and talking all day long."

Back in elementary school the teachers had the kids read stories in the classroom. Each person would read a paragraph and then it would go on to the next person. Dave suffered massive anxiety and counted how many students would read before him, so as to determine which paragraph he would have to read. "I would look to that first word and agonize if I was going to have problems getting that out of my mouth. When it came my turn to read, I would look calm, but my mind raced a million miles an hour and my heart pounded because I was having such a hard time with that first word."

It was at Pioneer High School that Hoffmann found that he couldn't overcome the stuttering, so he learned to deal with it. "If I had problems reading in school, I would blame it on my accent. I pretended that I was trying not to sound so 'Texan'. It was a little trick I used to avoid embarrassment."

On the freshman football team, embarrassment was tougher to escape. Hoffmann was the quarterback and middle linebacker. In both positions, he needed to call plays. As quarterback, he would huddle the team up and lead into the play call by saying… "Let's go get a first down……" or some other noise before telling his teammates what play was being run. They would laugh at him and he would laugh right along with them.

The following year, on the varsity, he played several positions, including backup QB. Once again, he had to make calls in the huddle. During practice, the coach stood a few feet away and would tell Dave which plays to call in the huddle. It was tough. The coach might say, "I-9-35 on two!", which was a simple power running play. Dave would make a throaty, guttural sound before calling the play. Guys in the huddle burst out laughing all the time and the coach once looked at him like, "*What in the world was that?*"

"I couldn't help it," recalls Dave. "Standing before my teammates, my attitude was, 'Hey guys, I have an obvious problem here. But if you want to laugh, then laugh, but whatever.' It was a thorn in my flesh. I read in the Bible where St. Paul says that a thorn in the flesh, we don't know what it is, but it serves to keep us humble. I realized that stuttering was my thorn. It forced me to be confident. You grow a confidence when you have something that you have to work through. It's almost like a disability; there's not always a way around it."

But when it came to playing football, there were no problems; just incredible fun and joy. Dave never played quarterback much, but when he did it was memorable. One day, the starting QB turned his ankle and the offense was handed over to Hoff. Dave ran a lot of bootlegs and counters and the offense marched down the field. When they got down to the six-yard line, Dave turned to center Jimmy Orlowski, who was one of those squatty guys that was 5'6" x 5'6". Hoff told him, "The coach called a sweep play, but I'm putting my head into your back and we're going into the frigging end zone!" Orlowski nodded his head.

They lined up and Hoffmann took the snap and put his head into the squat center's back. The pile of humanity began to move. Hoffmann and Orlowski trucked with everything they had. Hoff kept churning his legs. When they were finally taken down, the guys pulled Dave up, and he saw that they were ten yards deep in the end zone. He and Jimmy just looked at each other and smiled. If they hadn't been stopped, they would've ended up in the parking lot.

That was also the day that Dave Hoffmann threw the only pass in his "quarterback career". As it happened, his thumb was severely sprained. He rolled out and tried to throw, flinging it 35 yards down-field but also about 35 yards up into the air. It got picked off. Funny thing was, Hoff sprinted down there and speared the defender, causing a fumble which Pioneer recovered for a net 20-yard gain. At the bottom of the pile, he and his Samoan buddy, Andy Maloata, looked at each other and laughed hysterically, shouting, "Hey, whatever works!"

The most memorable assistant coach at Pioneer was a lively little Italian guy, Coach Ragoni, who helped lead the freshmen team. "He wore gold chains and enough aftershave to kill a horse," Hoffmann says. Ragoni would tell the kids, "When the clock strikes three, you guys better be out there stretching regardless of whether we're there yet or not!" So Hoffmann would be down there doing a hamstring stretch, and even though his eyes were trained on the ground, he would suddenly smile and think "Rags is here!" The players could smell him from across the parking lot. They also didn't think Ragoni ever wore underwear in his life. "He would stand there giving us a pre-game speech with one leg up on the bleachers," Hoffmann says. "It was one of those things where you go, *You've got to be kidding me, man!*" Those big marbles sitting there, and all of us fourteen year old kids are going *What in the world is that?* We didn't hear a word he said—we were scared to death looking at that! He was a great guy, didn't mean anything by it."

During his sophomore season, Dave's biggest concern was his weight. In terms of height he had reached 6', but remained skinny. He talked to his parents about getting protein powders like other guys at school were using, but Mr. Hoffmann said they couldn't afford it. Mrs. Hoffmann overheard this exchange, and advised Dave to pop an extra couple of potatoes into the microwave and keep eating. Both parents preached patience and assured their son that his body would fill out more as he grew older.

By his junior year, Dave had gained 25 pounds and was up to 200 on a 6'2" frame. He was quite broad in the shoulders with a narrow waist and thin legs. He was stronger and faster and that season proved to be his best one yet. His reputation was growing as a hard-hitting linebacker. With primal intensity Hoffmann worked out daily in the school weight room. He loved the feeling of full fatigue that came from expending every ounce of energy and focus he had to give. While mopping his face and still laboring to breath, he'd step outside into the warm California air and take in his surroundings. In San Jose there are mountains to the east and west of the valley. Dave would look to each set of mountains, and then down south to Salinas and up north to the Bay, and he'd swell with fresh air and vow: "I WANT TO BE KNOWN AS THE BEST LINEBACKER AND HARDEST HITTER IN THIS VALLEY!"

Friend and Pioneer teammate Brad Transue was already a believer. There's one play he'll never forget from a Friday night game. "Me and a teammate tackled the ball carrier near the sideline," Transue recalls with a chuckle. "Dave came up and hammered all of us and drove us out of bounds, and broke the first down marker. Here you think you're the one making the play, and suddenly you realize you're just going along for the ride."

Pioneer played occasional night games at the San Jose Junior College. Players from San Jose State and guys from the city college would come out to watch the high school games. One night, Hoffmann had a monster game. Interceptions, forced fumbles and knocking multiple quarterbacks out of the game. Afterward, the Pioneer team walked off the field and past the chain link fence. Some college players were gathered close and there was a perceptible hush. "I could see that they were all looking at me," Dave recalls. "It felt good and I knew I had gained something."

But Dave Hoffmann was about to gain something greater. Heading into his senior season, Jerry Hannon stepped down as Pioneer's football coach to become the school's athletic director. The new coach he hired was Dan Lloyd. Dave had heard that Lloyd was once a bad ass linebacker for the Washington Huskies in the 1970s, and later with the NFL's New York Giants. Lloyd's tragedy came when, on the verge of NFL stardom, he contracted cancer of the lymph nodes after his fourth professional season in 1980. It almost killed him, but he survived. Still, in an era where the Giants would have future Hall of

Famers Lawrence Taylor and Harry Carson, Lloyd would have been part of one of the greatest linebacker corps in history. Nevertheless, his heroic attempts to come back from cancer led him to playing in the USFL—a miracle when you hear of everything he went through.

Lloyd's arrival at Pioneer came at an ideal time for Dave. They quickly developed an easy rapport and could talk football for hours. "He was the perfect guy to coach me," Hoffmann says. "Coach Lloyd would teach me more in the next year than all my other years combined."

CHAPTER 3

WHEN DAN LLOYD ARRIVED at Pioneer, Dave Hoffmann was bouncing off the walls. Being a former NFL inside linebacker, Lloyd had played at a world class level. Dave watched old films of his games and saw what a hard hitter and bad ass he was. He couldn't wait to get started.

In the local paper, they quoted Lloyd as saying, "I've wanted to be a head coach and I'm excited about my opportunity at Pioneer. The school has some good athletes, starting with Dave Hoffman (sic), and I'm already optimistic that we're going to field a good team next season."

From the very beginning, Dave absorbed every lesson that Lloyd threw at him . "I learned from him every day," Dave says. "He helped me develop in so many ways. I give him lots of credit for his care and wisdom. Dan Lloyd always speaks his mind, and some people don't like it and some people do. I like it, because I like him. In my eyes, he was a leader and a hero."

That leadership showed itself during fall camp. Lloyd would take the team to a nearby steep hill that was about 150 meters to the top. The kids would put on cleats and sprint all the way to the top. You had to keep sprinting, because if you slowed down, you would end up bear crawling due to the steepness. Dan Lloyd would lead the pack. He was in the best shape. Dave would smile and think *"This is great! Not only does he lead by word but also by example."* It was around then that Dave wished he could have played linebacker alongside him. But he was grateful for the one season they were going to have together as player and coach.

The feelings of appreciation were mutual. "Dave was everything I wanted to see in myself," Lloyd recalls years later. " A perfect player, perfect attitude, perfect linebacker. When someone is that receptive, you can give them more information and have a closer relationship than with some of the other kids. It was a linebacker working with a linebacker, and that lent itself to great chemistry that was working for us."

Lloyd's appreciation also stemmed from his pupil's propensity for ferocious hits. One day at practice, a bemused Lloyd walked over to Hoffmann and motioned toward the sideline. Dave looked over and saw the bench occupied with guys holding their heads and icing their necks, following collisions with the linebacker. "Why don't you take a break and do some stretching," the coach said.

Lloyd may have loved hard hits, but he knew where to draw the line. Dave didn't, and still had some maturing to do. One day in practice they were running a warm up drill. A tight end crossed the middle and the quarterback overthrew him. Hoffmann laid the guy out, just filleted him. He didn't think anything of it and walked back to the huddle. Lloyd walked over to Dave and whispered in his ear, "Hey, you don't have to be an asshole."

"I knew what he meant and nothing more needed to be said," Hoffmann recalls. "Coach Lloyd was saying that this is more of a warm-up drill, not a scrimmage. There was a time to tag a guy and a time not to. This wasn't the time. He was also saying, 'I already know you can stroke guys. You don't have to prove anything to me. It's time to grow up a little bit.' I got the message. To be a vicious guy, you don't have to be a jerk. From then on, I still hit guys, but only when appropriate."

Coach Lloyd also taught him ways to improve his linebacker technique. One day, they ran a scrape drill. Dave was scraping inside out on the running back and not giving him a cut back lane, but maintaining a high level of speed and a great angle to inflict a vicious tackle. Lloyd took Dave aside and taught him that instead of taking right angles it was best to take more of a direct angle. "You see a lot of linebackers take jumpy steps while they read a play, but those steps are a waste," Dave says. "Every millisecond you waste not attacking the play, the offense gains the advantage as they know where the play is going. Learning how to take that direct route to the ball made a big difference. That skill helped me for the rest of my career. Lloyd taught me the basics of that in fifteen minutes."

Hoffmann was a quick learner and found his anticipation becoming almost unbearable during practice. He was thinking, *Wow, I can't wait for that first game so I can unleash this!* Finally, the season opener arrived against Branham. Dave applied everything just as Lloyd had taught him— and he was a wrecking ball out there. Screaming past would-be blockers, making tackles for loss and inflicting vicious hits upon ball carriers. Dave's heart burst with joy every Friday night. .

But his senior year wasn't all fun and games. A pulled groin left him hobbled and in pain. Lloyd actually gave him his truck and Dave drove himself to a nearby treatment facility. For a few weeks, his practices were more like walk-throughs. That was Lloyd's experience at work there. Most other high school coaches would have had their star linebacker out there going full tilt and would have likely damaged further his groin. Coach Lloyd treated Dave like someone older.

"The best word for that situation was empathy," Lloyd says years later. "It was more important about what he was going to do later than what he could for me at that moment. There was no point in rushing it and not having it come back right and making it worse. There were things that people at Washington wanted me to do, or things that people in high school wanted me to do, and it wasn't worth it to play through some painful injuries I had. I wanted to handle Dave's situation with empathy."

Lloyd actually wanted the linebacker to sit out a couple of games, but Hoffmann insisted on being out there. As the season progressed the young linebacker discovered how to play in spite of the pain. Pioneer was just a decent team that year, but featured a stingy defense.

Dave smiled a lot that season. Pac-10 teams had been recruiting him heavily. Hoffmann scheduled official trips to UCLA, Cal, Arizona, Arizona State and Washington. USC seemed turned off that Dave wasn't able to come down and watch one of their games. He never did hear from them after that.

One school that intrigued him was the University of Washington. Their defensive coordinator, Jim Lambright, was coming down to Pioneer to visit him. Lloyd knew Lambright from his Washington days and spoke highly of him. Lloyd talked about the Huskies but didn't try to steer Dave toward them. When Lambright arrived, Hoffmann and him hit it off immediately. "We were alone in the coach's office," Dave says, "and Lambright looked at me and said 'I like you most because you're nasty.' That was key for me, because we both appreciated the violent aspect of the game and could talk about it honestly."

Soon afterward, Washington's legendary head coach Don James traveled to San Jose and paid a visit to the Hoffmann home. He stayed for an hour and the conversation never did center on football. Dave didn't say ten words. He just sat and listened. James discussed the Shriners' Hospital and what some of the kids there had been through and how they were helping them. He also talked about his Christian faith. Dave looked at him and thought, "This is a real man. He wasn't like a lot of coaches who are like used car salesmen. Don James cares about things that matter." On his way out the door, Don James turned to Mrs. Hoffmann and said, "we would like your son to come to the University of Washington." The coach then walked to his car and Mr. Hoffmann didn't say much afterward. But Dave could see that dad approved.

"Dave was coached by one of my former players—a great player—Dan Lloyd," recalls Don James. "Dan was really high on Dave and so we had good vibes on Dave going in. Every home we went into we absolutely did research. I remember that Dave's father and grandfather were Lutheran ministers. I grew up a Presbyterian but when I married Carol she was Lutheran, so I had a little background on their faith. It was a good visit."

When Dave took his official recruiting trip to Washington, he landed at Sea-Tac Airport for the first time in his life. He saw Husky Stadium, with its 72,500 seat capacity and twin cantilever roofs hanging over the grandstands. Next to the stadium was the Tubby Graves building. That's where he encountered fellow recruit James Clifford. James was a local kid and a big-time recruit at inside linebacker. The two came together like magnets. They vigorously shook hands and looked each other in the eye, and that was that. Best friends with no questions asked.

It was unusually warm that weekend and the group of recruits puttered out onto Lake Washington aboard a fancy boat. One of the prospects was an unheralded defensive tackle named Steve Emtman. In Dave's eyes, Emtman was a sight to see. He was a farm boy from Eastern Washington, sitting there in his blue jeans and boots and with a scowl on his face, looking to Dave like a kid who just had his lunch money stolen. Years later, Emtman laughed upon hearing Dave's description of that day. "I don't know about having a scowl on my face like I had my money stolen," Emtman says. "If anything, I was probably getting ready to kick Dave and James Clifford's ass for being so damn cocky".

Dave returned home Sunday night and told his mom and dad that he was going to Washington. Mr. Hoffmann asked him if he wanted him to call the other colleges and tell them the decision had been made. "I thought that was a great move," Dave says. "Dad knew I wouldn't be talked out of my decision, but that it had been a long and stressful process. When I told Coach Lloyd I was going to be a Husky, he was excited for me but said I should have taken all my trips for the experience. But I had no regrets.

"Any player will tell you that when you make your commitment it is a great feeling. In some ways, it is the first major decision a teenager can make. For me, I fell back on my faith and asked the Lord for His guidance. I asked Him to show me where to go and that I would trust Him. The people I met in the recruiting process and the incredibly strong feeling the Lord put in my gut, some call it instinct, made it very clear: I was meant to be a Husky."

Letter of Intent Day came in early February, 1988. A banner day at the Hoffmann home. Mrs. Hoffmann cooked up a breakfast feast. Several former coaches arrived, including Jerry Hannon, who had coached Dave during his sophomore and junior years, Dan Lloyd, and basketball coaches Steve Seandel and Todd Buller. Dave thrilled at seeing Seandel, who had made the long drive from where he was now an assistant at Santa Clara University. Seandel always stressed playing as hard and smart as possible, and coached with an intensity that Hoffmann found refreshing.

With everyone gathered around the table, 17-year old Dave Hoffmann signed on the dotted line. Applause broke out. He looked up and could tell his dad was proud.

Soon after, Dave received one of the most meaningful gifts of his life. He retains it among his valuables to this day. Dan Lloyd handed him a card. Inside, he had hand-written:

Hope everything turns out right.
Good luck!
Dave,

As this breakfast shows, you are off to a fine start and surrounded by many people who support and admire your efforts. Having your great athletic ability is wonderful and a gift; but as you expand your horizons, many competitors will have your ability and more. The difference, I believe, is in effort. Always give more than asked and lead with a purpose. Work hard on the dark rainy nights ahead and remember what is important to you and your family. I am looking forward to your Husky career.

My words,
Dan

CHAPTER 4

AS 18-YEAR OLD DAVE HOFFMANN walked with his family down to the curb, the Chevy Astro minivan sat waiting. Dave looked at his mom and dad, and brothers Matt and Steve, while a faint flicker of anxiety came to life in his gut. They were standing outside his new dorm at the University of Washington in Seattle, in August 1988. Farewells were being said as the Hoffmanns prepared to return home to San Jose, less their eldest son. One by one, Dave shook hands and gave hugs. He tried hard to show he was a grown man. Mrs. Hoffmann's last words to him were, "We're proud of you David. May the Lord bless you."

Dave didn't feel scared or homesick until about fifteen minutes after they drove off. Says Hoffmann: "I was thinking, *Wow, I am not going to see them tonight for dinner. I'm not sure when I will see them again.* It started to sink in, like lowering oneself into a cold bath. *Man, this is different and I'm not sure I like it.*"

Dave's surroundings were suddenly different. He arrived in Seattle when the city was at the cusp of a fascinating time in its history. Microsoft was becoming a worldwide force in the computer industry. 18-year old Ken Griffey, Jr. was about to debut with the Seattle Mariners. The local comedy sketch show Almost Live! was wildly popular. And grunge bands like Nirvana, Soundgarden, Alice in Chains and Mother Love Bone (the pre-cursor to Pearl Jam) were about to explode onto the world stage.

The family rituals defining Dave's life were now 1,000 miles away.

Praying together before meals, daily chores, horsing around with his brothers and hearing his mom call out "Good night Dave" across the house when we went to bed.

He was living his dream of playing major college football, but the knot in his gut would not go away. In the coming weeks it proved the worst in the mornings and at night. While lying in bed, his mind raced with anxiety and his heart was heavy with sadness. He often tossed and turned, knowing he needed to get to sleep.

"I knew he was really homesick and me and my family reached out to him and tried to help him through everything," said roommate and teammate James Clifford. "But it was something he had to get through." Dave longed not only for his family, but for his tight-knit group of buddies back home.

"Hitting it off right away with the other freshmen helped eased some of the pain," Dave says. "But James Clifford's family treated me as one of their own. From the start, I felt like I had known James for years and years."

The hot weeks of August training camp led up to Washington's 1988 football season. For Dave, some of those days were brutal. He wasn't the biggest guy in the world, standing 6'2" tall and weighing 205 pounds. That would be a good size for a safety, but undersized for a Division I linebacker. It was tough enough putting on weight. But at this point, he was just trying to *maintain* his weight. Part of that came from the grueling double day practices they currently endured upon the scorching Husky Stadium turf. But it also stemmed from homesickness. The players would eat breakfast at the nearby Crew House overlooking Lake Washington. Dave ate what he could despite his churning stomach. As the meal concluded, the players would rise from their tables and head out the door and across the lawn to get taped up for team meetings and double day practices. On certain days, Dave ambled along, grieving for home, furtively eyeballing nearby shrubbery. He'd lag behind, letting his teammates get out ahead of him. Then he'd dart behind a targeted bush or tree and throw up breakfast. He'd pause for a moment, hunched over in humility, absorbed in deep sadness, before gathering himself and pressing on to rejoin his teammates.

His days soon became so filled with homework and football that he learned how to utilize every moment of every day and not waste time. Being so busy during the day helped ease the homesickness. "Things that wrenched me emotionally would get put on the back burner because I was taking care of business," he says. "But it was in the quietness of the night that I would miss home. At the same time, I wanted to make my family proud. I wasn't going to quit. That wasn't an option. There were freshmen on our team and all over America that were going through what I was going through. I just had to keep going. I had faith that I was doing what God wanted me to do. I was not going to jack with the plan, and quit to take the easy road. That just wasn't an option."

Prayer had played a big part in Hoffmann's decision to go Washington. It prevented him from worrying about it much. "I knew who was really running the show," he says. "I just needed to be aware of that and give thanks to Him. I was going to go to the school I was supposed to go to. I was beginning to learn the concept of leaning on Him. To look upon God as a wall that I could lean on with everything I had and know that it will never give. It takes faith to extend oneself like that. I was learning that there was satisfaction in knowing I was where I was supposed to be."

Despite the homesickness, Hoffmann was fired up because he could see that they had a special group of guys in the incoming player class. He met guys that had the same intensity and passion as he did. He felt like he had known them all for years. "We were made of the same stuff and had the same goals," Hoffmann says "People talk about how special college football is and they are right. Players are from all over and are just busting their asses to get better and get through school. But great teams have guys who automatically look out for each other. It is more than a brotherhood. We didn't know how much success we were going to have, but we were aware that we had something special. These guys all busted their tails and we spoke the same language. It was about action. We weren't about saying what we were going to do, we were about doing it. Proving it to each other every day that 'I'm the guy you want next to you in the trenches.'"

Among the incoming class on defense, only James Clifford would be playing right away. The coaches redshirted Hoffmann and the others. This meant that they wouldn't see the field until the following year. Hoffmann and fellow freshman Steve Emtman quickly bonded. They commiserated in their frustration in not being able to play right away. "We were freshmen who weren't playing and we were angry," Steve Emtman recalled. "There were times in my freshman year that I thought things were screwed up and that the coaches were screwing me over. It's kind of funny how you remember the little things, but I remember calling my dad to do a little whining and get a little sympathy. He was like, 'Well work harder.'"

Of course, the first time the Huskies traveled for an away game, the redshirting freshmen had to stay behind. Emtman had a car, and he and Dave climbed in and drove to Emtman's hometown of Cheney in Eastern Washington. They humored themselves by bitching into an audio recorder in their finely honed professional wrestler dialect, complaining of how they should have been on the traveling team and how they were going to prove the coaches wrong. Then they'd play it back and laugh at how ridiculous they sounded.

However, during practices, the freshmen scout teamers hit it as hard as they could. "To the older guys on the team it might have just been practice," Hoffmann says, "but we were getting it on. Our offensive coordinator Gary Pinkel and the other coaches screamed at us all the time. We gave them headaches. But if we were going to be out there then we decided we were going a million miles an hour. It was the start of something. We were the rag tag scout team, a bunch of freshmen, raising hell on the practice field."

Following an season opening win on the road at Purdue, the Huskies opened up their home schedule against the Army Cadets. Dave could only stand by and watch as his buddy James Clifford got to play right away. "James got earholed on the opening kickoff," Hoffmann recalls. "His pupils were dilated. Blood was running out of his nose like a faucet. He was just laughing hysterically. He said: 'That guy got me!' Like James always does, he just jammed gauze up his nose and it did the trick."

"I'll tell you exactly what happened," James Clifford recalls. " I was a true freshman and it was my first home game. I had told Dave and Emtman and all those guys to watch me this weekend—I was going to kill Army! We kickoff to start the game and I'm L4 or something like that, right on our sideline. 76,000 fans in Husky Stadium all amped up. I'm boring down the sideline to make the tackle. I should have had my head on a swivel, but I didn't of course. Out of nowhere this little Army guy comes out and absolutely decleats me. Right from the side, I never saw him coming. Knocks the piss out of me. I fly into the sideline. Right at the feet of Dave, Steve Emtman and all those guys. Blood's running out of my nose. I jump up and I'm high fiving the guys all fired up and screaming, like I just freaking made a touchdown. Everyone was looking at me like *what the hell is wrong with you?*"

Clifford's intensity was not limited to the football field. Up in their seventh floor dorm room, Cliff and Hoff used to have vicious games of Tecmo Bowl on Nintendo. "These were some heated games!" says Hoffmann. "Many things got broken and I'd be lying if I said James and I didn't throw things around the room. One time after I intercepted one of his passes, he chucked his entire playbook out the window. We sat there in silence for about fifteen seconds and then ran out the door. We figured the elevator wasn't fast enough so we sprinted down seven flights of stairs and ran out into the rainy night. We searched all the bushes until we found every page."

Later on, Hoffmann roomed with teammates Mark Brunell and Todd Bridge. He became close friends with both of them as well. Mark Brunell laughs when remembering those early days with Hoff. "Todd Bridge had his stuff in his room, and I had my stuff in my room," Brunell says. "Todd had his stuff and it was all organized. I had a dresser with posters and pictures on the wall, and Husky stuff, all organized. The only thing Hoff had in his room was a mattress on the floor. That was it. Nothing on the walls, no dresser. Just a mattress on the floor. That was kind of fun. If he tells you anything different, he's lying."

"Well, I did thumb tack a couple of small pictures of my family on the wall," Hoffmann says. "But otherwise it's true. It was a huge California King mattress that I had gotten from the Cliffords. They were about to throw it away. It was huge and I don't know how I got it through the doorway, it almost filled the entire room. I didn't have room for furniture. But if I did have some, it would have been built out of milk crates from Emtman's house."

"People liked being around him though," Brunell says. " Everyone had a lot of respect for Dave. Some were even a little afraid of him, as he could be an intimidating person. He had the linebacker mentality. You always knew when Hoff Daddy was around. Lots of energy. But you always had to be cautious about getting him too fired up. You never knew when he was going to suddenly take you to the ground and rough you up. I was his roommate and one of his best friends, so I knew that better than most. Most people know how to play and wrestle and have a fun time. But when Hoff Daddy was wrestling, something was going to hurt. You weren't going to leave the wrestling match laughing and having a good old time. He was going to win and he was going to hurt you. Nothing malicious of course, but enough to rough you up a little and let you know that he was the boss."

Wary teammates knew the warning signs. Dave would grit his teeth and forge a big happy smile. The guys would start going, "Hoff... Hoff... easy there, easy!" Out of desperation, they might even resort to the trick Mrs. Hoffmann taught them, and pat his shoulder while telling him to cool his jets. Sometimes that worked; more often it didn't. Especially if someone violated one of Dave's sacred rules, like watching commercials, which he proclaimed off limits in the apartment. The way he saw it, with the convenience of remote controls, why in the world would someone watch them? Hoff figured everyone could be entertained or educated by something else more valuable while waiting. But once when Todd Bridge broke the covenant by watching a commercial, an apoplectic Hoffmann launched himself at Bridge like a jungle creature and took him to the floor. "He nearly pierced my ear with his teeth because we had watched a commercial," Bridge recalls. "Commercials were completely off limits. Never saw a commercial in the two years we were roomies. Never watched a TV show in its entirety for that matter."

When raising the issue of physical attacks upon those around him, Hoffmann shrugs. "It's my way of pouring energy and love in an intense way into something I care about." he says. "I'm a physical guy."

This is not to paint him as an out-of-control maniac. A junkyard dog attacking every passerby. No, it didn't happen so much in the locker room, but usually at home around his buddies when he hadn't had his daily fix of smashing somebody. He had long recognized that he had a different level of intensity than most others. But when he arrived at Washington and met guys like Donald Jones, they connected in a special way. Jones may have grown up in Virginia, but Dave regarded him just like a brother. Jones had the same intensity, passion for the game, work ethic and good-hearted nature.

"The main thing with Dave Hoffmann and me was always our spiritual connection," Donald Jones says. "It was a strong love and bond. Our interactions were probably a little different than his interactions with some of the other guys. We were always using scripture to pump each other up because we were both walking with Christ. We would say, 'In the name of Jesus we can do all things through Christ!' We would quote scriptures and that would light a fire under me. Dave knew how to motivate people. He knew how to motivate me. He knew what got me fired up, and that was the word of God."

The word of God was what brought former Husky Mike Rohrbach back to UW around that time, when Don James offered him the team chaplain position. Rohrbach had been a captain of the 1978 Rose Bowl Champions — the team that shocked the college football world by stunning heavily favored Michigan. He was currently chaplain for the NBA's Seattle SuperSonics and thrilled to add the Washington Huskies to his duties.

Rohrbach and Hoffmann hit it off immediately. Two common denominators greased the skids: Hoffmann played high school football for Rohrbach's beloved old teammate, Dan Lloyd. Hoffmann was also wearing Rohrbach's old jersey number 54, and that made the new chaplain smile.

"We called it *The Magic of the 54,*" Rohrbach says. "Go ahead and laugh about it, say whatever you will. There was an initial bonding. More than that, it's the brotherhood of Husky linebackers. I had been where he was. He was an up-and-coming stud on the scene. I loved his spirit. And then I found out he was a Christian. As team chaplain, it thrilled my heart that here was a quality young guy that God could use mightily to encourage the hearts of others."

Rohrbach at that time was state director in Washington for the Fellowship of Christian Athletes. He ran a huddle group on campus at the U-Dub. Hoffmann immediately became involved along with teammates like Mark Brunell, Orlando McKay and Todd Bridge. They were all vocal leaders. "Hoff had a real heart for caring for other people and wanting them to be a part of FCA and the Bible studies and Fellowship groups," says Rohrbach. "He cared and was compassionate toward others, just like Christ would want us to be."

Rohrbach was married with a budding family and Hoffmann viewed him as an older brother. Their conversations revolved around life, football and faith. Rohrbach favored the 1 Corinthians verse: *Do you not know that in a race all the runners run, only one receives the prize, therefore run in such a way as to win.* In future years, this passage inspired Rohrbach to found the youth outreach program called Run to Win.

"Man, we're in this race to win," Rohrbach says. "The scoreboard is important, and God says so, in his words. He wants us to be fierce competitors. And the thing about Hoffmann, that guy had a warrior mentality. When he took the field, he put it on, and he put it on people. He was out there honoring God through his play. He was never trying to be malicious or hurt anybody, but he definitely wanted them to know they had come into his area, and he was on patrol... Yes, Christ wants us to be compassionate, loving, caring, humble. But the Bible also says do your work heartily as for the Lord and not men. He wants us representing Him. In Ephesians, it says to put on the full armor of God; suit up! When I think of Hoff, there's a guy who flexed his spiritual muscles. There's a guy who let it all hang out. There's a guy who played every game with the intent of honoring God and putting on display the gifts and abilities that God had given him"

By the end of the '88 season, Hoffmann and the other freshmen may have been highly motivated, but team-wide motivation was on the wane. The Huskies slogged across the finish line with a 6-5 record. The brutal Apple Cup loss to the Washington State Cougars demoralized everyone associated with Husky Football. The Cougs were going to a bowl game while Washington wasn't— for the first time in a decade. Husky fans thought the world was coming to an end.

"There was a feeling like some of the older guys on the team were happy the season was over," Hoffmann says."All of us younger guys said, 'This isn't why we came to Washington!' We knew we only had so many years to make something happen. The way things were going, we almost weren't surprised by the loss to Wazzu. It's like some guys were just trying to survive instead of dominate."

With the season over, the players gathered in the team room to be addressed by Don James. "It was the most amazing thing," recalled Steve Emtman. "You've got a bunch of 18-20 year old guys in the meeting room, talking loudly and carrying on. When that man walked into the room, it was instant silence. You didn't even think about finishing your thought."

James strode to the podium. In the past year he had already made changes to his recruiting practices, with increased emphasis on speed over size. Now in the wake of an unacceptable mediocre season, he was bringing the water to full boil.

"We knew there needed to be a change," Hoffmann says. "We all felt it and wanted it. When Coach James told us that we were going to get after it, to get faster, more intense, more physical, we already knew it, but it was good to hear it from the head of the lion. Words like that need to come from somebody credible, and Don James was credible.

"The guys in our class didn't need a bunch of pep rally talks, we were motivated from within. We left the meeting and knew that when we got back from Thanksgiving break we were going to get to training. I knew I was with the best quality guys and excited for the days ahead. It may sound corny for me now to say that we knew the future was bright, but we really felt that way."

CHAPTER 5

HOFF RETURNED HOME TO San Jose that summer of 1989. He was happy to be home but his waking moments were consumed with thoughts of Texas A&M coming to Seattle in early September. It would be the first action of his Husky career.

Those hot summer days combined equal measures of hard work and fun. Dave trained as hard as always to get stronger and faster. But he worked a summer job—that wasn't an option. Mrs. Hoffmann insisted on that. Since the age of twelve, Dave always had jobs in the summer. In previous years he worked at stores, shops and toiled for landscaping companies in the hot California sun. However, this time around, he got a job as a delivery guy for a lighting company. "I drove all over the Bay Area delivering light bulbs," he said. "What was great about that job was that it didn't zap me. When I worked landscaping or unloaded furniture for Levitz Furniture I was always drained at the end of the day. But as a delivery man, I didn't feel wiped out. I had lots more to give in the weight room at the end of each day."

At Pioneer High School, they had a classic old gym with brick walls and pipes running through the ceiling. In other words, Hoffmann's kind of place. The familiarity proved comforting and seeing Dan Lloyd regularly gave Dave extra motivation.

Dave's brother Steve was heading into his junior year at Pioneer and was becoming a force himself on the line. Through June and July, the two brothers trained together intensely. By that point, Steve had grown taller than Dave, well on his way to standing 6'6". But Dave still called him "little brother", and both of them wouldn't have it any other way.

The brothers would go out to a dirt track alongside the high school. They'd take Dave's old Chevy Blazer, which had a brush bar on the front of it. Dave had realized that the angle he was at while pushing it was the same foreword lean he got into when striking a lineman on the football field. So he and Steve took turns pushing the blazer back and forth along the track, while the other piloted the steering wheel. As they pushed and dug with their every ounce of strength, they exercised all the muscles from their toes to their shoulders and triceps.

"After doing it a few times, I decided that instead of pushing it for long periods of time, we would push it for 60-70 yards at a time and at full speed," Dave said. "Going as hard and fast as possible helped us to mimic the intensity of a football play. We wore our cleats to keep from slipping on the dirt. We would keep our head down while pushing, and whoever was steering would countdown out loud for the final five yards so we knew when to stop. After that doing that drill a few times there was no shame in throwing up behind the bleachers. You had to push yourself to get to that level of a workout. Some old high school teammates tried it with us, but none ever returned. That told me that it was a pretty damn hard workout. Not just physically, but mentally, it's good to put yourself through ordeals like that to get ready for the season long battle and grind. I always liked knowing that our opponents weren't doing stuff like that."

But it wasn't all hard work—the Hoffmann boys had fun too. After finishing with work and training, they'd head to the family backyard to what they called "Club Hoff". Friends would come over and they'd jump in the Dough Boy swimming pool and spit watermelon seeds and have some All-American fun.

Dave originated the term "Club Hoff". The Hoffmann house was close to the high school and friends were always coming over to hang out. Some of Dave's Husky teammates came down that summer for a few days too. Sensing the need for structure, Dave created a board of directors. "I appointed my brother Steve as the *Secretary of Da-Fence*," Dave says. "His job was to make sure that nobody unauthorized got into the back yard. My other brother Matt was vice president. Dad was the 'Owner' and mom was the 'Official Mom'. Of course, I named myself president.

"We had a deck that was right next to the Dough Boy pool," he says. "Guys without trunks would drop their drawers and jump in with their skivvies. We often rolled watermelons out there and chopped them up and ate them while hanging over the side of the pool. Invariably, we'd smash the rinds over each other's heads. You would leave a half inch of red with the rind and sneak up on someone from behind and smash it right onto their skull."

If backyard shenanigans resulted in someone getting a gashed limb or bleeding scalp, Mrs. Hoffmann never missed a beat. A nurse by trade, she'd transform the family bathroom into a mini hospital ward. Jane's Clinic, they called it, as the patient took a seat upon the closed toilet lid, while Mrs. Hoffmann applied liberal doses of peroxide and butterfly bandages.

With the crisis averted, the walking wounded returned to the backyard to rejoin the others. Mrs. Hoffmann brewed jars of iced tea on the back step and Dave downed those by the quart. When it came time for BBQ ribs, Dave established and enforced a rule that no one was allowed to use a napkin until completely finished. Sauce would be all over the place.

His brother Steve relishes memories of the *Tour de Hoff.* "We had a bike race one day," Steve says."There was about thirty of us. We started by doing the Club Hoff jumping jacks to warm up, then we raced our bikes up to Colero Lake. Had a BBQ when we got up there. Just a lot of fun. When we got back home, I snuck up to the gym at the high school. On the side of the scoreboard there were places reserved for team members for the basketball team. I grabbed the letters and spelled TOUR DE HOFF and listed the top three finishers. When school opened on Monday everybody saw that and wondered what it was about. But the teachers left it up there for about three months. That was great."

By summer's end, Dave chomped at the bit to get back to Seattle and play football. In fall camp he proved himself to be stronger, faster and in the best shape of his life. No longer was he a member of the scout team—he had cracked the two deeps. The Hammer's time was coming.

On the Friday night before the season opener against Texas A&M, the Huskies traveled to the suburb of Bellevue to stay in the Greenwood Inn. That was a first for Dave, because scout team members don't get to partake in that while sitting out the year.

"Older guys on the team walked around the hotel and knew where they were going," he says. "The coaches told us that the defensive meetings were in the ballroom. I didn't know where that was, so I watched where the older guys were going and followed them. Afterward, I went to Mike Rohrbach's chapel meeting being held in a adjacent room. Seeing his familiar face was a welcome sight."

After chapel concluded, they issued the players a turkey sandwich, an apple, two chocolate chip cookies and a little carton of milk. Dave took his stash to his room and kicked back with his roommate and flipped channels.

He could barely contain himself the next morning. He gazed out upon Lake Washington as the team busses received a state trooper escort across the 520 bridge toward Husky Stadium. The dozens of boats sailing toward or moored before the stadium mesmerized Hoff with their beauty.

A couple hours later the Washington Huskies tromped down the tunnel and poured onto the field in front of 70,000 screaming fans. Dave was so jacked to finally be able to make a difference. With guys like Dennis Brown and Martin Harrison anchoring the defense, Hoffmann felt they couldn't have had better senior leaders.

"It was a real hot day at Husky Stadium," he says."I looked across at the Texas A&M players. It was interesting to see their maroon helmets in person— I had only seen them on TV while growing up in

Texas. We were going to kick off to start the game and I ran out onto the field. I was knocking helmets with some of my teammates. I took a quick moment to look around at the fans in the stadium and soak it in. But you know, it doesn't matter if there are 100,000 people in the stands or only 100 people back at Pioneer. Football is football and it's a beautiful game no matter where you are or how many people are watching."

The ball sailed into the air and Dave raced downfield like a predatory jungle creature. He arrived deep in enemy territory at a high rate of speed and hit an A&M blocker and collapsed the play. This forced the return man to bounce back into the middle of the field where Dave's teammates combined on the tackle. "I had really laid a shot on the guy and it felt great," he says. "Me and my teammates were jumping on each other as we ran back to the sideline. I took off my helmet to get a drink of water, and there were maroon streaks on my helmet from the A&M guy that I hit. I hadn't had enemy colors on my helmet since high school."

With Keith Gilbertson as Washington's new offensive coordinator and senior Cary Conklin at quarterback, the Huskies built a 19-6 lead and carried it deep into the fourth quarter. With just a few minutes left, Coach James determined the game to be out of reach.

James and assistant coach Randy Hart started waving and shouting for the second stringers to get ready for action. "They held us back like bulls about to run down the street," Dave says. "When the shout came for the twos, we sprinted onto the field and screamed at the ones 'Great job! Way to go!'"

Hoffmann soon got a taste of what he loved best. The Aggies threw a little dump pass to a receiver in the flat. Dave came up and planted his forehead into his back, knocking him to the hot turf. "It felt good!", he says. "Having your buddies jump on you and celebrate big plays was great. And after the game, walking up the tunnel and into the team room feeling a little beat up and seeing the streaks on my helmet and the plastic-coated metal on my facemask chewed up... Well, I just wanted more."

CHAPTER 6

THERE'S AN OLD EXPRESSION about needing to learn to walk before you can run. Approaching the middle of the 1989 season, that was exactly the state of the Washington Huskies. With a 2-1 record they would now host the Colorado Buffalos. National scrutiny was on this game, due to off-the-field circumstances. Sal Aunese, Colorado's would –be quarterback for that season, had died earlier in the week from cancer. Adding to the drama was the fact that he had fathered a child with the daughter of Bill McCartney—Colorado's coach.

The Buffalos entered Husky Stadium heavy with emotion, running onto the field and taking a knee en masse at midfield to point to the heavens to let Sal know they were thinking of him. Once the game started, they proved to be at an elite level and far beyond Washington. Running the option with wild abandon, the Buffalos consumed yardage in giant chunks and ran the ball down Washington's throat all game long.

In the third quarter, with the game out of reach and the Husky Stadium crowd thinning out, somebody on Washington's sideline yelled, HOFFMANN GET IN THERE! "Man, I was pumped," Dave says. "Playing the run has always been my best attribute, and I did pretty well. I got good reads, played aggressively and was hitting the fullback in the backfield."

But nothing could save Washington by that point. Colorado destroyed the Huskies 45-28, and it wasn't that close. It proved to be the worst home loss in Don James' UW career. However, Hoffmann felt the team learned from that game. "Colorado taught us what it took to be a big-time team," he says. "We knew we had great players but we weren't playing as a unit. We were playing on our heels. Bend but don't break, keep everything in front of you. We didn't yet have the scheme that would fit just like a glove to our hand."

Early the next week, Hoffmann's eyes got big as he gazed upon the wall and found his name listed among the starters for a road game to USC. The Los Angeles Coliseum served as a grand venue for a redshirt freshman making his first start. Hoff stuck his nose in there and created violence at the line of scrimmage. And UW freshman safety Tommie Smith made his presence felt, blocking a Trojan punt and then recovering it for a touchdown. But Rose Bowl-bound USC fended off the Huskies 24-16, which was Washington's third loss in a row.

The Huskies kept searching for answers. They bounced back with wins over Oregon and California. Then they traveled back to Los Angeles for a game against UCLA. The Bruins jumped out early to a 21-0 lead and by the second quarter were leading 28-7. Things looked dire for the Dawgs, but the team refused to surrender. At one point, Hoffmann struck a lineman and shed his block, then snapped the Bruin ball carrier and caused a fumble. Steve Emtman recovered, and this led to a Washington score. A little later, freshman Husky linebacker Jaime Fields picked off a pass and once again put Washington in scoring position. In the game's final minute, Greg Lewis took a handoff on a draw play and score from ten yards out, giving Washington a 28-27 win. "We noticed that the younger guys were starting to heavily contribute and make a difference," Hoffmann says. "We were no longer thought of as younger guys, but just part of the team."

A terrible home game a week later against Arizona State became the final catalyst for transformation. ASU quarterback Paul Justin shredded the Husky defense for 490 yards. The Sun Devils won 34-32, dropping Washington's record to 5-4. Once again, the Huskies staggered toward the season's finish line.

The following week, Don James and Jim Lambright gathered the players together in the team room and announced that they were transforming the defense into an attacking gap defense. Defensive backs would be using much more bump-and-run, single man coverage. Defensive linemen would get up field and penetrate the backfield and not worry about the linebackers, who would take care of themselves. Lambright exhorted them, shouting "Let's get after it!" The players responded with big smiles and high fives.

The Huskies traveled that week to Corvallis for a night game against the lowly Oregon State Beavers. Lambright moved the athletic Donald Jones from fullback to linebacker, and Donald immediately shined as a terror off the edge, racking up three quarterback sacks. Middle linebackers James Clifford and Dave Hoffmann raised hell at the line of scrimmage. Oregon State's offense was overwhelmed. The Husky players reveled in the results of the 51-14 win. "We felt, 'alright we've got something here. We can be something special,'" Hoffmann says. "We had fun. You could tell because we were jumping on each other and getting lots of tackles for loss."

The Huskies concluded the regular season a week later with a 20-9 win at home against the WSU Cougars. Washington, at 7-4, clinched a berth in the now-defunct Freedom Bowl. "The defense was slowly coming together," Hoffmann says. "We had all the right ingredients but needed to put it all in a bowl and mix it together and put it in the oven. The aggressive attack scheme fit us perfectly because it matched our attitude in practice and in the weight room."

Since the previous season, the Washington coaches had been recruiting faster and more aggressive players. Now, James and Lambright had altered the defensive scheme to fit with the more aggressive mentality. That mentality showed itself primarily in the weight room. "I looked at the weight room as a chance to become a more devastating player," Hoffmann says. "I wasn't mesmerized by lifting totals. I was a strong guy but not the strongest guy. But when I was down on the bench press, squat rack or doing power cleans, I fantasized about opponents. I wasn't sitting there dreaming about how I looked in the mirror. I had a nasty mindset in the weight room, and most of the guys did. We had some really strong physiques, but our purpose was to be great football players.

"Lots of guys focus on a number in their head that they want to bench or squat," he says. "My thing was being able to be more devastating on the field. Of course you set goals for yourself, but you know what? When I heard a guy bragging that he just benched 550 pounds and thought he was king of the jungle, I loved drilling him right in the sternum and dropping him. I let that be known. While training is important, it's all just a means to an end. Ultimately, it's about the overall attitude. I would rather have guys with a kick ass workout and then dominate on the field, than someone who bench presses a lot and can't play the game. When you break huddle and walk up to the line, does anybody care how much you can bench press? Nobody cares. You may have guns the size of Texas, but unless it helps you become a road grader, put those things away and let's do something that works."

Washington's new attack style fit in well with the frenetic manner that the team practiced. "When you were a Washington Husky back in those days, you never walked," Hoffmann says. "You ran on the field. You ran to your drills. When your series was done you ran off the field. If you slowed up even one step before reaching the sideline the whole defense would be running extra. To most other programs that would seem extreme, but for us it was expected and common. When we scrimmaged against the scout team, there were two or three offenses on scout team that took turns. After we finished a play, the next offense would break huddle while we were running back into position. The reason wasn't for a no-huddle experience, but for getting in as many reps as possible. We got in more reps in one practice than most teams got in an entire week."

Multiple scouts came in from different NFL teams and told coaches and onlookers that they'd never seen a college team practice like that since the days of Bear Bryant at Alabama. "That was a badge of honor to Coach James," Hoffmann says. "It took a toll on our bodies, but if we had to do it all over again we would do it the same way, because it's what set us apart."

The UW players knew they needed to find ways to make those grueling practices light-hearted and fun. "We all had a few screws loose so it was easy to joke around with each other," Hoffmann says. "You hear players these days complaining that it's tough and they're not having any fun. Well, quit your bitching and make it fun. Make it a good time. That's what we did."

The players on defense would come up with a "Word of the Day" and use it as much as possible during practice, producing such ridiculous results that sometimes the fatigued players were laughing hysterically. On the occasions an offensive lineman grew irritated by an undersized defender like Chico Fraley yapping his trap, he'd amuse himself by grabbing Fraley and rag dolling him. "At times I didn't know a bad fight from a good fight," recalled Fraley. "But I knew that I had those guys behind me, especially Hoffmann and Clifford. They came to my defense on a regular basis. It's easy to pick a fight when you know who is on your side. It was a Lambright mantra, that if one's in we're all in. We all had each other's back." Hoffmann recalls those skirmishes fondly... "That was a lightning-quick reaction," Hoff says. "You could see it and smell it when it was coming. So we were usually in there giving somebody a shot before they even got to him or were able to do much. We were in there laying shots. To say we had each other's back was an understatement."

Why the players maniacally had each other's back stemmed from the intense teachings of defensive coordinator Jim Lambright. During practice he regularly had a rule where all eleven players had to touch the ball carrier. Say linebacker Brett Collins shot the gap and made the tackle. He would hold the guy down and wait for his ten teammates to arrive. Lambright also stressed that they were playing football because it was fun. He said they all worked too damn hard to not celebrate when good things happen. So if someone got an interception or recovered a fumble, no matter where the others were on the field, they had to run to their teammates and celebrate. The players would jump on each other and bark like rabid dogs.

During an exhausting practice this wouldn't always be welcome. Linebacker Chico Fraley recalled the time when cornerback Walter Bailey made an acrobatic interception on a long bomb down field. "He fell down after catching it," Fraley says. "We had to run about forty yards down the field to go celebrate, but we were muttering amongst ourselves, *Damn it, Walter! You're supposed to run those back!*" This sometimes pushed the players to their physical limits. So they discovered a loophole: When a player made a big play during a scrimmage, his ten exhausted teammates would run to him and form a big scrum, leaning on each other and jumping up and down. They'd hold that position for as long as possible in order to catch their breaths, until assistant coaches came charging in with whistles blowing and shouts to stop celebrating.

From up in his tower overlooking practice, Don James never caught on to the ploy. Down on the field, Lambright never sniffed it out either. When informed two decades later, Lambright burst out laughing. "I guarantee that if I realized that's what was happening I would have jumped all over it," he says. "But the whole point of that was that you got players winning together and celebrating big plays and getting used to being the first ones decorating the person who just made a great play. When you develop that mentality and get players celebrating with each other, you get to a point where players who will run a long ways to be a part of it and you never get quite enough celebrations in your life like that."

Heading into the Freedom Bowl, the newly attacking Washington Huskies felt revitalized and definitely in a celebratory mood. They were much further along in their metamorphosis than opponents realized. With a pedestrian 7-4 record, nobody was talking about them. There was plenty of media attention, however, about their opponent. The Florida Gators had a disappointing season, but they had their All-American running back Emmit Smith. Maybe Florida wasn't excited about going to the Freedom Bowl and made it clear they weren't concerned about the Huskies. But Washington appreciated the invitation, since they hadn't gone anywhere the year before. Plus, it was the first bowl experience for the young starters, including Hoffmann. The chance to be in the Southern California sunshine and go to Disneyland and other team activities was a welcome gift. With game time approaching, the Huskies felt like they were going to get after it.

UW staff up photos of Florida players on Husky players' lockers. Mug shots of the player each Husky would face the most during the game. "I tore mine down," Hoffmann says. "I took it as an insult. I never cared too much what my opponents said or did. I created my own thoughts of my opponents. I never needed any extra motivation to get ready. I was already pissed and ready to go."

When the Freedom Bowl kicked off, the Husky defense stunned Florida right away. The Gators quickly grew shell shocked by their inability to move the football. "I noticed something about their offensive linemen," Hoffmann says. "In the Pac-10, it was a pro style kind of play. They hold you in tight. We were taught to snap the blocker and separate. But Florida didn't do that; they just fired off and tried to push you, more like what you see in high school. I remember thinking that this Emmit Smith guy must be great to have gotten so many yards with blocking like that."

Against Washington, Smith rushed for a mere 17 yards and became so frustrated that he pulled himself out of the game in the third quarter and never returned. The Huskies won 34-7, and finished the 1989 season with a three game winning streak and an 8-4 record. The future looked bright and Dave Hoffmann and his teammates couldn't wait for 1990.

Just before the snowball fight with brothers Matt and Steve.
Our first and probably last Texas snow day.

Reuniting with my family after bowl practice.

Hoffmann brothers after Rose Bowl practice.
Christmas at the beach.

Day before the Rose Bowl with some of my best buddies,
Mark Brunell and Todd Bridge.

Having some fun in the Duck backfield.

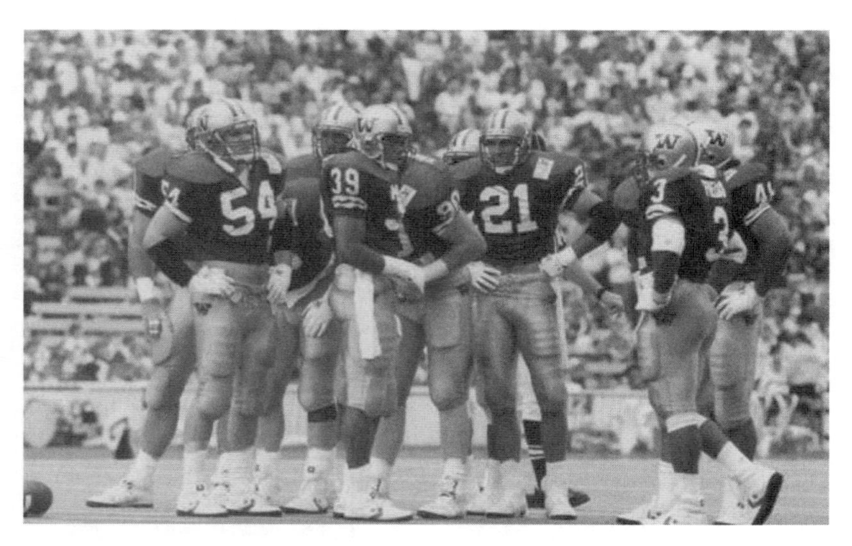

Our band of brothers in our cherished spot,
the defensive huddle.

Defensive Coordinator Jim Lambright had us so well prepared we couldn't wait to get out there.

Rose Bowl eve with Lambo and Cliffy before our third and last Granddaddy of Them All.

Standing at midfield of the Rose Bowl
with quarterback Mark Brunell.

Just before the snap in the Apple Cup
with the fearsome Don Jones.

Captions at the coin flip. Feeling ornery and excited.

Calling audibles and pointing out tips to each other
to gain an advantage.

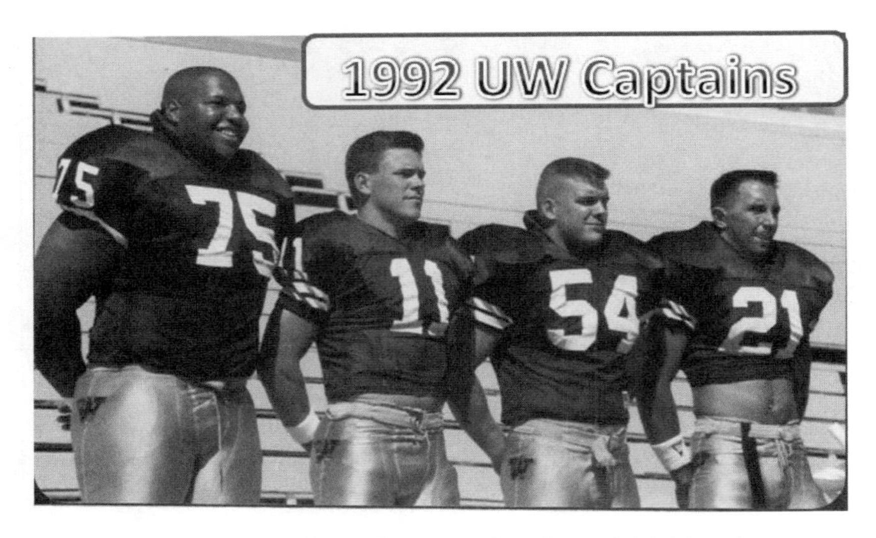

The captains of the 1992 squad: Left-to-right, Lincoln Kennedy, Mark Brunell, myself and Shane Pahukoa

After warm-ups of our third Rose Bowl in 1993 with my backer brother, James Clifford. I wore his cleats during our 1991 Rose Bowl when he was out with knee surgery.

With my parents, Paul and Jane Hoffmann.
So thankful to the generous Butkus Award committee
for bringing out my Mom and Dad to Orlando, FL.

Butkus! What a blast!

Old Dawgs at Spring Game reunion. With running back Eteka Huckaby and Little Bro Steve.

20th year reunion of National Championship team. Here's our linebacker crew, from left to right: James Clifford, Chico Fraley, coach Jim Lambright, me, Brett Collins, Steve Springstead and Hillary Butler (kneeling). The late Jaime Fields is in the photo behind us, and always in our hearts.

At the reunion with my dear friend,
the unstoppable Don Jones.

On air being interviewed by former quarterback Hugh Millen
on the UW Campus.

On the sideline of Husky game with my former teammates. Always love seeing those guys! Back row, from left to right: Eteka Huckaby, James Clifford, Tyrone Rodgers, Chico Fraley, Steve Emtman. Front row, from left to right: Me, Walter Bailey and Greg Lewis.

Brother Steve and I with Don James, before the championship team presentation, November 2011.

CHAPTER 7

WELL-RESTED AND TANNED FROM two summer months in California, Dave Hoffmann returned to Seattle with adrenaline pumping for fall camp. Since the win over Florida, the Huskies felt like something special was brewing for 1990. Especially on defense, with guys like Hoffmann, Steve Emtman, Jaime Fields, Shane Pahukoa, Tommie Smith all being sophomores, while James Clifford, Donald Jones and Dana Hall were juniors. Tyrone Rodgers, a transfer defensive tackle from Oklahoma, was eligible to start. For senior leadership, guys like Travis Richardson, John Cook and Eric Briscoe were stalwarts in terms of toughness and ability. "Travis in particular was really tough and had a confidence about him," Hoffmann says, "and that helped set the bar for the entire defense. John Cook was a hard-nosed defensive lineman and very consistent. He helped form the attitude for the entire defense."

As fall camp started, Husky players could sense the friendships had deepened. They ratcheted up their effort and worked in unison to get better and support each other. Backup running back Eteka Huckaby cited Dave Hoffmann as a galvanizing force.

"Hoff symbolized the spirit and toughness of the team," Huckaby said. "During practice you could always hear him talking to teammates. He had this way of encouraging you while he was smacking you in the face with his one of his signature hits. He would run around practice with bounce in his step, sometimes imitating pro wrestlers, mainly Hulk Hogan and Randy 'Macho Man' Savage. So you would often hear a collision, followed up with an OHHHHH, YEAHHH! or... YEAH BROTHER! Since I was one of our main scout team running backs we constantly went head up. We'd smack pads and after a good thud, his face would light up, and OH, YEAHHHHH BROTHER! would echo through the empty stadium. After practice in the locker room, he would come up to me and with a wink and a smile would say, *Did you feel that today brother?*"

But fall practice wouldn't be without setbacks. Especially during one scrimmage, right there on the Husky Stadium turf. James Clifford, who led the Pac-10 in tackles as a sophomore, blew his knee out. Someone fell and knocked his legs sideways. Everyone heard his blood-curdling scream. "My eyes still get watery thinking about that moment," Hoffmann says. "When you hear the scream of someone you love, it's brutal. It hurts to hear any teammate go down. I can still remember good friends blowing out their knees and breaking their legs and screaming. It's horrible. James is like my brother, and to hear him scream was something I'll never forget. It was tough to get back in focus after that. But you have to. I tried to use my anger about his injury and my love for him as focus and energy, instead of getting depressed about it, which you could easily do."

Clifford declined surgery, focusing instead on returning for the USC game, which was the season's third week. Whether that was overly optimistic remained to be seen.

Meanwhile, Washington opened the season as heavy favorites against San Jose State. 66,347 fans settled into Husky Stadium expecting a continuation of the Freedom Bowl massacre from the previous season. Husky fans also loved great defense, and linebacker Jamal Fountaine recalled a play from that day that energized the home crowd into a barking froth.

"This San Jose State running back was running the ball," said Fountaine. "I tackled him and was holding onto his leg and he's dragging me a bit. I'm trying to wrestle him to the ground. Suddenly behind me I hear someone screaming for about five seconds...

AHHHHHHHHHHHHHHHHHHHHHHHH!!!!!!!!

"Hoffmann comes up and knocks this dude out of bounds, and they both knock over the guy over who was holding the yard marker, and then they smash into the water bucket. All that was left of my attempted tackle was the running back's shoe in my hand. I looked at the guy and was like, *Yeah, you're jacked up. You should have just gone down when I tackled you instead of getting blasted by Hoff!* So I'm standing there with his shoe and I didn't know what else to do— so I just flung it at the guy."

But Washington's offense, led by sophomore quarterback Mark Brunell, sputtered for 60 minutes. It was thanks to Beno Bryant's 52-yard punt return for a touchdown late in the fourth quarter that enabled the Huskies to squeak by, 20-17.

When Washington traveled the next week and edged lowly Purdue 20-14, one thing became clear: The Husky team that crushed Florida was nowhere to be seen. UW fans and media began fretting over whether sophomore quarterback Mark Brunell could lead the team. His growing pains were symbolized from a play late in the first half against Purdue, as the Huskies went into their two minute offense.

Brunell's head swirled with so much information to process. Scanning the Purdue defense, he lined up to take the snap from guard Dean Kirkland. Center Ed Cunningham burst out laughing along the line of scrimmage. Brunell realized his error and then lined up properly. "You're looking at five big butts on every play," Brunell said later, "and they do look alike."

While the fans and media doubted Brunell, the UW players didn't. "I had full confidence in Mark and it was kind of an unspoken thing," Hoffmann says. "Something about Mark that people didn't know is that he was a tough guy with strong faith. He's a guy you want to go to war with."

But now the real gridiron war drew near. It was time for the Centennial Celebration and a home game against 5th ranked USC. The Trojans were the three-time defending Pac-10 Champions led by Todd Marinovich, who was widely considered college football's best quarterback. The game against USC would cap off a week- long celebration as the University of Washington celebrated 100 years of Husky Football. Coach James asked the players to have our game faces on all week and avoid distraction. The primary question was the health of James Clifford.

"At first I decided against surgery," Clifford recalled. "I was going to rehab it. I wanted to be back for the USC game. The year before I had 27 tackles against those guys. Everything was good and I was ready to get my position back. Tuesday of that week we were doing 9-on-7 drills. Probably the hardest drill we did. Lots of hitting and it's all inside run—it's ones against ones. I stepped out of it. I said, 'I'm good. I don't need to do this. My knee is good. I don't need to do this drill.'

Hoffmann approached his friend. "Cliffy, you need to do this."

"What are you talking about?"

"You've got to find out, man. You need to find out if your knee is ready or not."

"So I enter the 9-on-7 drill," Clifford recalled. "First play I blew up the running back. Everything was great. Next play, I hit the running back and a lineman fell on my leg and my knee brace shattered and my knee totally blew out. I was laying on the ground screaming in agony. It wasn't just from the pain, but also because I knew the year was gone. That I was done. I had surgery a few days later."

The team was momentarily shaken by the incident. "James really tore up that knee," Hoffmann says. "If he wasn't as tough as he was, there's next to nobody that would have been out there practicing like that to begin with. He was trying to get through the practice and do just enough. But here we are about to play USC, and he had to know if he could play on it. Up to that point, he hadn't pushed it, changed direction, or done much with it. I think in the back of his mind he knew it was already torn. I asked him if it was game ready. I was over playing the backer spot, and if he wasn't ready I needed to get back over and practice the MIKE linebacker spot. So he needed to know if he was truly ready to go."

That Friday night at the Crew House, former Huskies spoke to the players. Warren Moon, the quarterback and MVP of the 1978 Rose Bowl, was one of them. "That meant a lot," Hoffmann says. "All the guys in our era appreciated and respected the Huskies that came before us. Whether it was Hugh McElhenny, Rick Redman, or some of the younger guys that played more recently, they all got our full respect when they came to our sideline during practice or in the weight room. When those guys spoke to us they weren't using index cards, they spoke from their hearts. They believed in us. USC was the king of the Pac-10 and guys like Warren Moon believed we could take the crown away from them."

The next day, in those precious moments before kickoff, Don James said some last words and led the Lord's prayer. Coming down the tunnel toward the field, Hoffmann felt like a gladiator entering the arena. "It was on," he says. "The tunnel was dark and loud, and packed with players. We had our Say Who? chant bouncing off the walls. When I reached the mouth of the tunnel, it was instant bright light. The noise and light hit you all at once. The crowd's roar was like twelve freight trains rolling right on top of you, deafening in a beautiful way. We got the signal to go and we exploded from the tunnel. The energy of the fans carried us onto the field. I was out there with my buddies and I was ready to get it on. I soaked in the stadium atmosphere for a few seconds, said a prayer and prayed that we would kick off. Our crew was ready to play some nasty defense."

The stadium was electric amid 90 degree temperatures and blue skies above. Early on, Hoff sacked USC quarterback Todd Marinovich, and received instant turf burns up and down his arm from the scorching hot turf. "I really felt alive right there," Hoffmann says. "Jumping up and down with my teammates and having a great time."

Washington's plan against the elite USC offense was revolutionary in its way and surprised the Trojans. "The whole idea there was to send more people than USC could block," recalled defensive coordinator Jim Lambright. "To overwhelm a quarterback who was beyond phenomenal. It was about how much pressure could we bring and where we could we bring it from. And it worked."

The Huskies built up a 24-0 first half lead. Each time USC's offense broke huddle, an embattled Marinovich approached the line of scrimmage with a look of bewilderment in his eyes. Lambright trusted that the defense had the athletes to cover on the edges and allow the linebackers to blitz and attack with abandon. "Physically we were stuffing the run," Hoff says. "Even though Marinovich had the arm, USC was still known for running the ball down people's throats. To completely stop them from doing their strong suit gave us more confidence, and sent us deeper into a feeding frenzy. We became like a bunch of sharks fighting over a piece of meat, and jumping all over each other after the whistle. When you watch film of that game, you can see how much the guys all loved each other."

"Right before halftime one of my teammates got a sack and my finger got underneath Marinovich's gums," former defensive tackle Steve Emtman said. "He was bleeding. It was funny to see him looking all dazed and confused. Then we're heading up the tunnel and their running back Ricky Ervins is talking crap. We were kicking their ass and he's running up our tunnel talking crap. He just didn't get it. After hearing that, there was no way we weren't coming back out in the second half and finish the job. We shouted at him, YOU'RE A FOOL! YOU'VE JUST MOTIVATED OUR WHOLE TEAM!"

The mayhem continued into the third and fourth quarters. The Husky defense toyed with the Trojans, blitzing and stunting and having the time of their lives. Meanwhile, the UW offense was enjoying a productive day. Running back Greg Lewis made several big runs, and quarterback Mark Brunell silenced critics by completing 12-of-23 passes for 197 yards and a touchdown. Washington prevailed 31-0. The USC Trojans walked out of Husky Stadium knowing they were no longer Kings of the Pac-10.

For Brunell in particular, it was the start of what became a brilliant career. "In the first two games I think Don James came pretty close to replacing me with Billy Joe Hobert," Brunell recalled. "Then came the USC game. I was very nervous and to be honest my confidence wasn't very high. But the USC game ended up being a turning point for me and the team. It was a special day that I will never forget."

Spontaneous cheers erupted from joyful fans as they exited Husky Stadium that day—the only time long-time Husky fans have witnessed that reaction. "It was the same thing for us players in the locker room," Hoffmann says. "We were still smacking each other and jacked up. The guys had a real mature thought process. We knew we still had a long ways to go. But we knew that we just did something big. It was a real moment of satisfaction. Beating USC 31-0 doesn't happen by accident. It was evidence that the hard work and sacrifice were paying off."

The locker room's happy chaos included James Clifford in street clothes. He and Hoff made eye contact and gave each other a big hug. "When you're that close you don't even need to say much," Hoffmann says. "There's just an understanding. We were both excited, but at the same time he hadn't been out there. I loved playing with Chico Fraley but it was a shame that we couldn't have all been out there together. But sometimes that's just the way life is."

Clifford had surgery the following week and missed the rest of the 1990 season. "Coming back from my knee injury was the hardest thing I've ever done," Clifford says. "In the weeks following the USC game, there were times when my knee wouldn't straighten out or was swelling. The whole team would have left the locker room and I would be in there sobbing. Because I couldn't physically do what I wanted to do or what I was used to doing. One guy would stay every night, man. I'm talking up to two hours after practice. Dave would be there with me. Sometimes he would just put an arm around me and not say a damn thing. Other times he would say, 'What are you worried about? You're better than everybody else. You'll get back out there!'"

Those trying times seared themselves into Hoffmann's memory. "We sat there many times after practice when the locker room was a ghost town and drips from the showers were the only sound we heard," Dave says. "When I told him I thought his best football was ahead of him I really believed that. His family was very loving and supportive of him and I was fortunate just to be counted among it's members. But that injury really did a number on him. It was bad. A lesser man wouldn't have tried to practice on it. James Clifford is one of the toughest guys to ever come out of that tunnel at Husky Stadium. At the same time, he is one of the nicest, greatest, most genuine guys you'll ever know. That is why I cherish my brotherhood with him and why he is such a great dad to his daughters today. People love being around him. But I remember those nights in the locker room. There was nothing more important than helping him through this time in his life."

CHAPTER 8

DESTROYING USC sent Washington's confidence into the stratosphere, and set the Pac-10 abuzz. The Huskies were 1-0 in league play and 3-0 overall. They felt like the sky was the limit. But were they as good as they thought? Could they get better with each passing week?

The next game served as a severe measuring stick. They traveled to Boulder, Colorado to take on the Colorado Buffalos. A year had passed since the massacre at Husky Stadium, and now Washington was a different team. "Folsom Field was a beautiful place to play and we gave them a battle," Hoff says. "They had a big fullback, a quarterback and tailbacks that could all run. It was ground and pound. Both teams really respected each other. They could see that we had come a long way since the previous year. There was a lot of slapping heads after plays. They appreciated and admired the way we were coming with it, and it came down to the fourth quarter."

With less than a minute to play, the Huskies trailed 20-14 and had the ball first and goal inside the Buffalo 10-yard line. But four incomplete passes later, the game ended with a Washington loss.

The Huskies felt like they had learned something and felt it very important to get back to a dominating mindset. Traveling to Tempe, Arizona the following week gave them the chance to play the Sun Devils in a beautiful, warm game on the grass. The Husky defense descended like a pack of wolves and Washington annihilated ASU 42-14. The following Saturday UW returned home to host #19

Oregon. After beating the Ducks 38-17, Oregon head coach Rich Brooks stated that in all his years of coaching he had never seen his own team so physically beaten up.

Now with a 3-0 record in the conference and 5-1 overall, the Huskies were climbing toward the top 10 in national polls. "Our defense started to feel like we could be the best defense in the country," Hoffmann says. "We truly realized that if we stuck to the game plan we could dominate every week. Mentally we were really getting into the opponent's offensive game plan and predicting what they were going to run. When that happens, and you get after it and gang tackle like we did, it really starts to build on itself."

Hoff couldn't wait for Friday, when the team would board a plane bound for a Bay Area game against Stanford. The old San Jose gang came out to see Dave and his Washington Huskies. His brothers Steve and Matt along with buddies from his Pioneer days. Pastor Paul Hoffmann brought a large contingent from his church to see the game, tailgating in the parking lot and hanging out on their own section of the grandstands. Dave hadn't heard from Dan Lloyd and wasn't sure if he would be there.

It was sunny and warm—the kind of day Hoff had reveled in since his boyhood days in Texas. From the moment the Huskies stepped on the field, they attacked Stanford quarterback Jason Palumbis from everywhere. The Dawgs attacked from all angles and asserted control from the moment they stepped on the field. Washington racked up nine sacks, including 3 1/2 by Donald Jones. They also picked off two passes and recovered three fumbles, one of which was scooped up and returned for a touchdown by roverback Eric Briscoe.

Washington won 52-16, improving its record to 4-0 in the Pac-10 and 6-1 overall. Stanford finished with 339 yards, but it got 136 of them in the fourth quarter, against Husky reserves. That was a "problem" that Washington faced the next three years. They would get so far ahead in games that the backups would come in early and the final stats wouldn't reflect reality. For example, at the end of three quarters against the UW starters, Stanford only had 29 yards rushing. By the end of the game they had 78. Even still, Washington now led the nation in rush defense.

One of Stanford's offensive linemen, Chuck Gillingham, later said that Washington had the most physical defense he'd ever seen. During the second half, Dave Hoffmann played a part in giving Gillingham that impression.

Stanford had the ball on the left hash and lined up in a passing formation. Ed McCaffrey, a talented wide receiver, went into motion just before the snap. Hoff saw him coming on a crossing route as Palumbis threw the pass. "I took a couple of steps and got full extension from my toes to my hips and caught McCaffrey with my forehead right under his chin," Hoffmann says. "The ball jarred loose and I knew that I caught him good. There was instant celebration with my buddies. He was lying unconscious in the fetal position for quite awhile and word was he didn't play for several weeks."

"I'll never forget that hit," says former UW linebacker Chico Fraley. "Ed McCaffrey made the mistake of running through the zone. Ed came out on my side. At Stanford there were about 12,000 people in the stands so it was easy for Dave to hear me clear as day. I passed him off as I was supposed to. Dave hit him so hard and I jumped over the top so I wouldn't get hit. As I was above them I looked down and Dave was completely through him. It sounded like a car wreck. Dave hit him with the crown of his helmet on the facemask. It was a vicious THWACK! Everyone knew that Ed was out the minute Dave hit him. I was very thankful I didn't try to take Ed out on that play or we would have both been lying there."

After stuffing Stanford on a fourth down attempt, the Husky defense ran off the field while mobbing Hoffmann. On the sideline, chaplain Mike Rohrbach shouted at Hoff as he approached and jumped on him as he crossed the boundary. Up in the press box, defensive coordinator Jim Lambright had a big grin on his face.

"Let me tell you, that was the greatest hit I have ever seen in all of my football life," Lambright recalled. "The receiver was knocked out cold in mid-air. It was one of those hits that I will forever remember.

Honest to God, I have never seen anyone hit harder than that."

After the game Hoff was coming up the ramp and saw his family and friends waiting. He had a few minutes to say hello before boarding the team bus. He hugged his parents, brothers and received back slaps and congratulations for the win. Suddenly, he spied Dan Lloyd and his wife Vickie. Lloyd was standing there with a big smile. Hoff grinned back as they embraced. Lloyd slapped him on the back and said, "Great job Stallion! Nice shots. You're using some of the things I taught you. I'm really proud of you!"

"It felt so good to get his approval," Hoff says. "To go out there in front of him and be an impact on the game was meaningful. For him to take the time to come out and see us play also meant a lot to me."

CHAPTER 9

THE REPRESENTATIVE FROM THE Rose Bowl made his way to the front of the team room while Hoffmann and his teammates settled into their seats. The players knew what was coming. The previous week the Huskies had crushed the Cal Bears 46-7, and now again at Husky Stadium, they'd just run roughshod over #23 Arizona 54-10, pushing their record to 6-0 in the conference and 8-1 overall. The game was an avalanche. Beno Bryant returned a punt 70 yards for a touchdown, then busted off a 73-yard touchdown run from scrimmage. Quarterback Mark Brunell connected with Mario Bailey for a 47-yard touchdown pass. The Huskies blocked two punts—one each by Jay Berry and Dana Hall. Even though Arizona had led the Pac-10 in rushing offense three years in a row, Washington's defense held them to 94 yards on 48 carries, an average of 1.9 yards per carry.

The representative officially announced to the room that the Washington Huskies were the 1990 Pac-10 Champs and would represent the conference in the Rose Bowl. Everyone cheered. Hoff turned around and looked at senior Travis Richardson, who had been a warrior and leader at defensive end. They hugged and jumped around like little kids for a few minutes. Dave enjoyed seeing him cut loose like that. The entire team was ecstatic. When Hoff was a kid he had dreamed of playing in a Cotton Bowl or Rose Bowl, and now it was going to happen.

The players weren't the only ones ecstatic. The coaches were too, including Don James. He hugged his wife Carol, and a few minutes later talked to the media and referred to the dominating way the Huskies were winning games. "Only the old Oklahoma and Nebraska teams used to win this way. It's a great feeling. It's a good group of guys who prepared well and hung in there week after week and put up some numbers that are absolutely incredible."

But two days later, there was suddenly more to play for, as evidenced by the Associated Press college football poll. Notre Dame was in the #1 spot, but the Washington Huskies had jumped from the #7 spot to #2 in one week. The nation was taking notice. The ranking was the highest for the Huskies since the 1984 team beat Oklahoma in the Orange Bowl.

Coming to Seattle the following Saturday were the downtrodden UCLA Bruins. The scene at Husky Stadium was one of rain, blustery winds and gloomy skies overhead. With a 4-5 record and several starters out due to injury, UCLA entered the game as a 21 point underdog.

In the first quarter, the Huskies ran a Red Dog blitz, sending all their linebackers. UCLA tailback Brian Brown popped through the rush and raced 88 yards for a touchdown right up the middle. That was the longest run ever against a Husky defense. On offense, the Huskies sputtered, with quarterback Mark Brunell having a tough day and running back Greg Lewis leaving early with an injured knee.

Meanwhile, Tommy Maddox was UCLA's redshirt freshman quarterback, and he did well with their shotgun formation. He threw a lot of short passes, unloading the ball before our pass rush could swallow him up. He completed 23 of 41 passes for 239 yards and two touchdowns.

Even still, Washington's Beno Bryant scored on a 3-yard run early in the fourth quarter, to give the Huskies a 14-13 lead. But in the game's final seconds, with winds swirling about the stadium, UCLA's Brad Daluiso 43-yard field goal attempt cleared the uprights to give the Bruins the stunning 25-22 victory.

Husky players were almost catatonic afterward. "That was a dark day for us," recalls Hoffmann. "Especially with the news that top-ranked Notre Dame had lost, meaning we would have been number one. I try not to mope and dwell on negative stuff, but there's no doubt about it, that day was rough." Added center Ed Cunningham: "It was the worst locker room I've ever been in after a defeat," he said. "It was highest to lowest. Not to take away from UCLA's great game plan, but if everything played out the same way it did that season except we won that game, we would have won the national championship. We were the best team in the country except that day. We were in such a haze afterward, none of us really talked to each other for three or four days. We were so disgusted, wondering what the hell happened out there? We 100% overlooked them. It's why coaches talk in clichés, that anyone can beat you at anytime."

"I don't think there was any letdown," Hoff says. "Defensively, there were some mental and physical mistakes we made on a couple blitzes and offensively we just didn't get it done. But UCLA had a great game plan with that short passing attack. A couple of screw ups we made ending up killing us. Because of the draws and short passes, it probably stopped us from blitzing as much as we would have normally. The whole time I thought we were going to pull that sucker out, but time ran out and we lost it."

The team regained its focus by mid week and traveled to Pullman for their last regular season game against Washington State. The young Drew Bledsoe was now leading the Cougar offense. The game was tied 3-3 after one quarter, but then the Huskies erupted for 52 unanswered points and won the game 55-10. "Wazzu went into shotgun a lot with no backs in the backfield with Bledsoe," Hoffmann says. "Whenever we saw that, we checked to automatic blitz." The Hitman registered two sacks, and overall the Huskies tallied seven. UW led 55-3 until late in the fourth quarter, when the Cougars scored a touchdown against Husky reserves.

Afterward the Washington players were happy but not ecstatic; it was more like a business trip. They'd finished the regular season with a 9-2 record, and were 7-1 in the Pac-10. Their opponent in the Rose Bowl was to be the big, corn-fed guys from Iowa. The end of the season awards came out and the Huskies made a clean sweep: Greg Lewis was Pac-10 Offensive Player of the Year, Steve Emtman was Pac-10 Defensive Player of the Year, and Don James was Pac-10 Coach of theYear. As a sophomore, Hoffmann led the team in tackles and was awarded by his teammates with the Chuck Niemi Big Hit Award.

Thanksgiving back home in San Jose provided Hoff a needed rest both mentally and physically, including a sore shoulder. Then all focus zeroed in on Iowa.

CHAPTER 10

AS SOON AS SCHOOL let out, Hoff couldn't wait to get back home to San Jose. Hanging out with the family did his heart good, as was sinking his teeth into a Thanksgiving feast prepared by Mama Hoff. A joyous mood permeated the Hoffmann home. Dave's brother Steve was now a senior at Pioneer, and was 6'6" and 240 pounds with colleges recruiting him heavily. "It was no secret that I wanted him to join me in Seattle," Dave says. "But I didn't say much. I didn't want to push him. It needed to be his decision."

Come mid December, the Huskies boarded a plane bound for Southern California for two weeks of preparation for the New Year's Day game against Iowa. "For entertainment, we had a blast down there," Hoff says. "Coach James always made sure to make bowl trips a reward for the players, considering the hard work we had given to the program. I got extra tickets and went to Disneyland twice; I was out there like a little kid running around." Hoff had also heard about the traditional prime rib dinner at Lawry's Beef Bowl. He saw photos of famous players and teams that had dined there in years past before playing in the Rose Bowl. He sat next to team chaplain Mike Rohrbach, and they devoured their prime ribs and put their plates on the bottom of the waitress's roller tray while her back was turned. When she looked back at them and asked if they wanted some prime rib, they replied, "Yes, ma'am!"

The team hotel was the Anaheim Marriot. Hoff enjoyed the luxurious atmosphere with the big illuminated pool. "I wasn't a big partier, so I had some pretty quiet nights. Many times, I walked over to the 7-11 in my flip flops in the warm air and got a big order of nachos. I took it back to the hotel and sat by the pool for a mini feast.

"Mom and dad couldn't be there with me for Christmas because dad was still a full time minister and needed to tend to church services," he says. "So I attended a Christmas Eve service hosted by Mike Rohrbach, and then me and some buddies went to the home of a family that was friends with my family. They took good care of us."

From Hoffmann's perspective, Don James never let up during the days leading up to the big game, but it was nice to see him relax in the evenings. "It was a side of him that we normally didn't get to see," Hoff says. "It was good seeing him enjoy his family. I might run into Carol James in the lobby or in chapel service, and she would ask about my parents. I liked seeing them in a different element."

The day after Christmas, preparations ratcheted up as the Huskies got ready to go to battle. As a Texas boy, Hoff loved practicing on grass fields under a warm sun. There were lots of high school kids and coaches from Southern California coming to watch them practice. Included among them was a superstar prep running back from Lompoc named Napoleon Kaufman. "It was fun to show them how we did it at Washington," Hoffmann says. "We did it like nobody else. The way we practiced and the way we got after it and hustled—it was fun to showcase that."

On the morning of January 1st, the Hitman and his teammates were sky high. Several hours before kickoff, they boarded the team busses and made their way to the Rose Bowl. Anticipation mounted as they drew closer to the venerable old stadium. The so-called Granddaddy of Them All. For defensive coordinator Jim Lambright, this was his fifth Rose Bowl as both a player and coach. "The team bus crests the hill that morning and you look down into the canyon at the stadium," recalled Lambright. "Your heart soars and tears fill your eyes. Then moments later you are standing on the grass, atop the painted rose, you're looking around and you know this is where you've wanted to be all along."

As Dave Hoffmann stood on the field during warm ups, the setting was the most beautiful he'd ever seen. From the painted turf, to the rapidly filling stands, to seeing WASHINGTON painted in the end zone and to looking up into the pure blue Pasadena sky. "The bands were going through their warm ups," Hoff says. "I looked up and found where my parents, grandparents and family members were sitting and gave them a wave. I thought back to my freshman year, when my parents dropped me off at the dorm and mom said 'You're playing with the big boys now.'" Now Dave Hoffmann was in the Rose Bowl, about to play in front of 100,000 fans and millions more on TV sets around the world.

Come time for kickoff, it was battle mode. "I got some solid hits on Iowa's big running back Nick Bell, and really showed their linemen how we did it at Washington," said Hoffmann. "They would try to block us and got a mouthful of helmet. It was important to send the message: *Hey, get used to this because it's coming all day!*"

The Huskies struck fast and furiously. Tommie Smith blocked a punt and Dana Hall scooped it up and ran it in for a touchdown. Mark Brunell hit Mario Bailey on a gorgeous pass-and-catch in the corner of the end zone for six. Charles Mincy picked off a pass and ran it back for a touchdown. The rout was on. Washington led 33-7 at halftime. The starters got pulled late in the third quarter and Iowa started a rally. "It made me physically sick to see them gaining yards on our backups and not being out there to stuff them," Hoff says. "Don James finally sent us back out there." The Huskies prevailed 46-34, but there was still a surprise in store.

"As the final seconds ticked off the clock we snuck up from behind Coach James and dumped Gatorade on him," Hoffmann says. "He turned around and yelled at us. We could see in his eyes that he didn't appreciate that at all. At that moment it seemed confusing and a bit uptight. Later in the locker room he apologized to us and explained that he had been battling pneumonia. I just recoiled and thought *That tough S.O.B. All this time he'd been battling pneumonia and yet he didn't tell anyone.* That man was 100% focused on our mission. That was the Husky culture back then and it extended to the players and entire staff."

"I thought I was dead," recalled Don James. "That's the most pain I've ever had. It wasn't pneumonia, but I had some sort of virus or flu with severe chills. When they poured that on me, it was a shock. I hadn't seen any reason to tell them that I wasn't feeling good. I had asked them to suck it up so I had to suck it up and keep going too. You know, do your job. Don't cry. I had that flash of anger because of the pain. But how can you be angry when you're going to win a Rose Bowl? You can't keep it that way. You get over it in a hurry."

The victory left Washington with a final record of 10-2 and a #5 national ranking in both polls. Mark Brunell and Steve Emtman had won game MVP awards. The team had a few days off. Dave went home to San Jose and spent time with family and friends. It felt good to take it easy for a moment and relax and reflect. But by the time he returned to Seattle for the start of the new school quarter, he was already fired up about the 1991 season. "With me, it's all about the hunt," he says. "I walked into the trainer's room to see what was going on. The coaches were out recruiting and it was our off season. I went over to the wooden roller cart with metal hooks where we hung our helmets. My old helmet was gone and a new one was on there. I went to the equipment manager, Tony Piro, and asked *Where's my helmet?* He told me it had cracked so they replaced it. I asked him where the old one was, thinking that I would like to have it as a souvenir. After all, I was the one who cracked it. I was the one laying shots on guys. But he said they cut them in half and put them on plaques to auction off at fundraisers. I thought *Holy smokes, man!* I used to go through a few of them every year and thought I could have had a heck of a collection."

However, all was forgotten when he stepped into the weight room to work out. He stopped dead in his tracks and gritted his teeth with a big happy smile. "The whole team was in there. No coaches or trainers had told us to be there. No one really even talked about it. It was the dark of winter and the season was many months away. Yet here we all were. It was beautiful to see."

CHAPTER 11

AS SPRING PRACTICE FOR 1991 commenced, players were running, hitting and blocking with increased vigor and spirit. Even absent the graduated Greg Lewis and Travis Richardson, the core nucleus of the team remained. That core nucleus worked out together, ate together, prayed together and verbally encouraged each other in the course of their daily routine. Even away from football, large groups of players would hang out. The battle-tested bonds of brotherhood bound these Huskies tight. With painful memories of the UCLA loss still seared into their psyches, the players vowed: *No letdowns this time around.*

One day, during a scrimmage, it was ones against the ones. Hoffmann dropped back into pass coverage with his back to the play, when he heard a scream. "I turned and looked," Hoff says. "Mark Brunell was in the backfield writhing on the ground and surrounded by teammates. Bru was hurt. Mark is an extremely tough guy and for him to not be able to get up meant the injury was big-time serious. Quarterbacks weren't supposed to be tackled during practice but this had been a simple accident. Later that day we heard his ACL was torn. Mark and I were living together at the time. He was such a great guy and a good friend and to see that happen to him devastated me. He was such a special piece to the team that it made me physically sick."

"It was surprising because those kinds of things aren't supposed to happen in spring ball," recalled Mark Brunell. "When it happened I knew it was serious. It was the most difficult thing I had ever gone through. Through it all, Dave was a true friend and very loyal. It was comforting that Dave was there. So supportive, so encouraging and so positive. There was never a 'That's too bad, what's going to happen to you?' It was always, 'You're going to get through this. Your best days of football are ahead of you.' He was a rock. Just a guy you could count on. There are lots of people that when things go bad they are nowhere to be found. Dave was the opposite. He always offered a ride at anytime or any sort of help I needed. He never let me down. It's one of the reasons we're such good friends today, because Hoff Daddy is going to be there through thick and thin."

"That injury tested Mark's faith," says Hoffmann. "He handled it incredibly well and was strong about it. He didn't go around and mope. He began rehabbing the knee instantly. Breaking up scar tissue and trying to heal from the surgery. He was going full tilt. He had that look in his eye that he was coming back better and stronger than ever."

In the meantime, Brunell's back-up was Billy Joe Hobert, a brash and untested sophomore from Puyallup, Washington. Hoffmann recalls those spring practice sessions with Hobert at the helm. "On the occasions when our first team defense scrimmaged against the first team offense, it was hard to judge how Billy would do because our defense was so dominant," he says. Given the stark circumstances, Husky fans and local media began fretting with worry. But each day, as the defensive players inhabited the locker room, the lone sentiment was: How can the defense become even more dominant? As Hoff had it figured, in the daily philosophy he espoused to everyone within earshot, *If the other team never scores, the Huskies can't be beat. And if the offense is struggling, then the defense will score a couple of touchdowns.*

When spring ball finished, Hoffmann returned to San Jose for June and July. His initial encounter with brother Steve erupted into bone-crushing hugs and backslaps. "My brother had signed with Washington was going to be a freshman for the upcoming season," Dave says. "It added great amounts of energy to our summer workouts, pushing my Chevy Blazer up and down the dirt track alongside Pioneer High School."

When asked about the 1991 season, Hoffmann says it's a simple story: "The defense went on a rampage that would not stop until they turned us off at the end of the season. Great players, hitters and preparers who loved and appreciated each other. Our goal was to destroy every offense that we faced. We made each game in 1991 a championship game. The coaches created a ladder made of poster board. There were twelve steps on the ladder, representing twelve football games. We only put the name of our next opponent on it; there would be no other names. Each game had the same meaning. Not a lot of fanfare, we were just going to get after it. We were taking every rung one at a time and loving every minute of it."

Right now there was only one visible name on the ladder—Stanford. The Cardinal had some talented players like running back Glen Milburn and Tommy Vardell at fullback. For the second year in a row, the game was being played in Palo Alto. From the very start, the Washington defense brought the pressure in waves and pounded away at the Stanford offense. Hoff knew from experience that after hitting a fullback for the first time they would spend the rest of the game chop blocking and coming in low. But after the first time the Hitman blasted Vardell, the Stanford fullback didn't change his approach. "Vardell wasn't going low; he was staying up high for our collisions," Hoff recalls. "During the third quarter, I gave him a big shot and jumped off and made the tackle on Milburn. I popped up and gave Vardell a high five and screamed THIS IS GREAT STUFF! He looked at me like I was crazy. It was the pure love of the battle combined with the fact he was staying up high. I didn't know if he was enjoying those car crashes as much as I was, but it was a lot of fun."

A large part of the fun came from the scoreboard: The Huskies crushed Stanford 42-7 and returned to Seattle with two weeks to prepare for the mighty Nebraska Cornhuskers and their legendary coach Tom Osborne. The national polls had Washington ranked #4 and Nebraska at #9. This game was being shown nationwide on ABC with the heralded Keith Jackson doing the Saturday night broadcast. This meant even Dave's relatives all the way down in Texas would be able to see it.

Because it was a non-league road game the Huskies got to bring a couple extra guys on the trip. The UW coaches made the determinations of which scout team players were practicing the best. "My brother Steve got picked," says Dave. "I was jacked! It was really cool to bring him on his first road trip. Both of our grandfathers were from Nebraska, and they were both attending the game. On Friday night after the team dinner, we went down to the hotel lobby and saw both sets of grandparents. They were there with friends of theirs who were wearing Big Red attire. I smiled extra big knowing they would be needling each other. Grandpa Meyer gave me a hug and told me the joke 'Do you know what the N on the Nebraska helmet stands for?..... Knowledge!' He had told me that joke twice a year throughout my childhood and I laughed harder every year."

The following night, coming out of the locker room prior to kickoff, the nighttime air in this Midwestern city crackled with electricity. The Huskies left the locker room and made their way toward the field via a concession area. "The ushers held up a rope so we could pass through," Hoffmann says. "Fans were standing there holding hot dogs and popcorn and yelling lots of fun things at us. They gave us an earful."

76,304 fans filled Memorial Stadium to capacity, and Don James later referred to the setting as a sea of red. It made an impression on Dave Hoffmann. "It was as loud as any place I've been," he says. "I could be standing twelve inches away from a teammate and we couldn't hear each other talk. It got even louder as Nebraska ran out onto the field. It was deafening. We didn't get intimidated anywhere we went. But we definitely appreciated the atmosphere and heritage that were in the air that night."

As Seattle Times columnist Blaine Newnham wrote, "If the

dream of a national championship were to die, this is where it should happen, against one of college football's great programs, at the feet of a shrine, on national television with Keith Jackson's sonorous voice calling the action as if this were some kind of world war."

"As someone who prided himself on stopping the run, I was really looking forward to attacking Nebraska's rushing offense," Hoffmann says. "The coaches had a great plan to use our speed, aggression and hitting ability to come off the end and disrupt things." An epic battle was underway in the trenches and both teams collided like two rams bashing each other with their horns. But things were going Nebraska's way. They built a 14-9 halftime lead. Then with 6:00 left in the third quarter, Nebraska punted and UW's Beno Bryant muffed the catch. The Cornhuskers recovered on the Husky 2-yard line, and moments later running back Derek Brown ran in it for the touchdown. Now the Huskies headed to the sideline trailing 21-9 amid a blast furnace of fan roar.

"For a quick second there, I had doubts," said UW linebacker Donald Jones. "I thought, *man we might lose this game.* Then Dave suddenly turned to me and shouted WE'VE GOT THIS GAME DON! That snapped me right out of it. Okay, we've got this game. Guys like Dave refused to lose. Refused to choke under pressure and adversity. Refused to choke under the brightest national spotlight. That's when leadership arises. He's a natural born leader and natural born winner. He brings out the best of the people around him. You hear that about people like Michael Jordan. I think of Dave like that, as someone who is an exhorter. If he sees you struggling he'll come over to see if he can help."

At about that same moment, Beno Bryant was sitting on the bench feeling distraught. "Everyone on the sideline kept coming up and shaking me and saying, 'c'mon, c'mon, it'll be okay,'" said Bryant. "Not one person said anything negative to me. Everybody was encouraging me. Then suddenly Billy Joe Hobert comes up and grabs my neck. He just looked at me and said matter-of-factly, 'We're not going to lose,' and then just walked off... That changed everything for me."

The Huskies needed points, and fast. The offense began to mount a drive. Hobert connected with Orlando McKay for a 33-yard touchdown pass, but it was called back due to a holding penalty that Don James disputed ferociously on the sideline. Now facing 3rd down and 27 from the Nebraska 49, Hobert scrambled up the middle for 19 yards. That brought up 4th down and eight yards to go.

"I made one change to the plan," recalled Don James. "We had moved the ball a bit, and while talking into the headphones I used that four letter word and said let's go for it. Gilby (Offensive Coordinator Keith Gilbertson) had already gotten up to go to the bathroom or grab a Coke and they had to call him back... I was just thinking how many more times are we going to get down there (in Nebraska territory)?"

A minute later came the moment of truth. Hobert dropped back then hit Orlando McKay with a thread the needle throw for 15 yards and a first down. Moments later, Beno Bryant scored on a 15-yard run up the middle for the touchdown. The score was now Cornhuskers 21, Huskies 16.

The Husky defense returned to the field and the intensity felt there was a screaming crucible. The coaches signaled in the play to Hoffmann and he turned toward his teammates to give them the call. "The huddle was a cherished place for me," Hoff says. "We were all prepared with our game plan. All tuned up physically and mentally to destroy an offense. The tension was big time. To be perfectly mentally clear in the middle of a violent battle is something I love. To make crystal clear, lightning-quick decisions while about to snap into a 315 pound lineman is awesome. Our huddle was a brotherhood of locked-on warriors who were away from the coaches, sideline and crowd— it was just us. The discussions in our huddle were always about giving each other confidence. Pumping each other up and reminding ourselves not to worry because we had each other covered. We had a bead on Nebraska's offense and each of us were beating the guy across from us. We felt urgency to find a way to win. I believed in my heart we were going to win. We were going to show these guys what we were all about."

The Huskies held Nebraska to three and out and forced a punt. Washington got the ball back and drove 69 yards in 8 plays and scored when Billy Joe Hobert connected with Orlando McKay for an 8-yard TD pass. The two point conversation failed, but the Dawgs led 22-21, with 11:20 to play in the game.

Two plays after the kickoff return, UW linebacker Jaime Fields blasted the Nebraska quarterback and jarred the ball loose. Paxton Tailele recovered for the Huskies. A few plays later Washington scored again when Hobert ran it in from one yard out. Again, the Husky defense went out and stuffed the Cornhusker offense, and on the ensuing possession UW running back Jay Berry ran 81 yards for the breakaway touchdown. Suddenly the Huskies led 36-21 and had broken the spirit of the Nebraska team, while amassing 618 yards.

Toward the end of the game, Hoffmann picked off a pass and ran along the UW sideline. He got tackled and was quickly engulfed by exuberant teammates. "I looked up and my brother Steve was there slapping the hell out of my helmet and then hoisting me to my feet," Hoff says. "That was a cool moment."

When the game ended, the jubilant Huskies began walking off the field, but came to a stop with looks of astonishment on their faces. "Several thousand Nebraska fans on a nearby walkway gave us a standing ovation," Hoffmann says. "You don't see that kind of sportsmanship every day. What gave me a lot of pride was that these guys from Seattle could go back to the Midwest and physically beat up the Nebraska Cornhuskers. They were known for being the bruisers. They were the real deal. But we were more physical. We were beating the blocks and outhitting them. Our machine ran better and harder than theirs at the end of the game."

Nebraska coach Tom Osborne fully agreed. "Washington's offense is good," he said. "Their defense is superlative. They compare with some of the very best, including Miami in the Orange Bowl three years ago. There will probably be a lot of good teams that won't come as close as we did tonight."

CHAPTER 12

IT'S NOT OFTEN THAT a stadium crowd gives a standing ovation during a 56-3 game. But that's what occurred at Husky Stadium on that last Saturday in September of 1991. Kansas State was in town and providing no resistance to Washington's onslaught. The lopsided results had lulled the home crowd into a subdued state. Then UW coaches told starting quarterback Billy Joe Hobert to take a seat. The familiar site of Mark Brunell suddenly appeared and jogged onto the field, moments from taking his first live snaps since the Rose Bowl win over Iowa. The fans immediately rose to their feet and exuded thunderous applause that acknowledged the magic of the moment. Less than six months after suffering a severe knee injury, Brunell had fought his way back onto the field.

A lot of people say they don't hear the fans when they're playing, which is true, except for moments like that," recalled Mark Brunell. "For me that moment was special. I wasn't expecting an ovation. I could hear the support and it felt good. To this day I remain appreciative of that moment because it meant so much."

From the sideline, Dave Hoffmann gazed upon the scene with his chinstrap unfastened and both hands on his hips. "I stopped and watched and soaked it up," he said. "I got chills. The band was playing some sort of Star Wars theme or some type of comeback music. I love the guy. It was cool to see—he was back. He was coming back to kick some butt. He was a great guy to have for team morale and chemistry. I would go to battle with Bru anywhere, anytime."

Brunell's comeback inspired the team and gave the offense two capable quarterbacks. But in that Kansas State contest, as well as the Stanford and Nebraska games, it was the defense setting the tone. The Huskies sacked the K-State quarterback eight times, including three by Donald Jones. The Wildcats finished with -17 yards rushing.

The Arizona Wildcats were the next rung on the ladder, coming to Seattle for an October 5th game at Husky Stadium. Washington had beaten them 54-10 in 1990. This year, head coach Dick Tomey believed they'd devised a plan to neutralize defensive tackle Steve Emtman and the Husky defense.

On the game's first two plays from scrimmage, Emtman stormed through the Wildcat line and sacked quarterback George Malauulu. Then he'd jump to his feet, lean way back with both arms extended and index fingers pointed skyward in his trademark pose of triumph. "It wasn't just Steve," Hoffmann said. "We were all just exploding on them. He happened to be closest to the ball and made great plays. The rest of us had beaten our guys and were there to hit the quarterback. But Emtman had beaten us to the punch. The mistake was thinking you could block Emtman at all. So of course you were going to give him a piece of your helmet because he stole your goods, he stole your candy. It sounds corny, but you would just be so happy for your teammate when they made a play."

When Arizona lined up for the game's third play, Malauulu looked over at the Husky linebackers stunting at the line of scrimmage and threatening blitz, while Emtman pawed at the turf like a raging bull—and Malauulu abruptly stood upright and signaled timeout. The Husky Stadium crowd erupted in exaltation. The opponent already seemed defeated and it would continue all day. Washington won 54-0, handing Arizona its first shutout loss since 1971.

The notoriety surrounding the Husky defense now extended nationwide, while the following joke circulated at UW booster cocktail parties:

Q: What's black, fast and has two white assholes?

A: The Husky Defense.

People looked at Steve Emtman and Dave Hoffmann as a tandem. This was largely due to their high-octane intensities. Emtman was a farm boy who grew up in Eastern Washington in the town of Cheney. Despite the different background, his hair-on-fire playing style matched Hoffmann's. "I loved him like a brother," Dave says. "He loved penetrating the backfield. When I saw him deep in the backfield I knew things were going well. Our front seven was often deep in the backfield. The scheme we played allowed our defensive line to make things happen and do a lot. Steve maximized that and made the most of it."

Former UW coach Don James was asked about Hoffmann and Emtman. "I think back to when I was coaching Jack Lambert at Kent State," James said. "One day he came in the office and said 'Coach, I know you worry about academics and eligibility, but worry about those other guys, don't worry about me. Because this is so important to me that I am going to make sure I'm eligible.' Both Steve Emtman and Dave were just like that. They were both good students, and you knew they were going to class and would graduate and would be eligible. You didn't worry about where they were during the nights and what they were doing. You didn't worry if their minds were in the game. They had the intellect, athletic ability and desire to be great. They were also great competitors. They would get mad with their teammates if they didn't do what they knew they should be doing."

The Dawgfather wasn't exaggerating. Hoff and Emtman's fanaticism zeroed in on teammates who weren't going 100MPH. During a drill, Emtman might deliver a ringing blow upside the head to a loafing player. Or given the right circumstances, a confrontation might occur. Once, when a defensive lineman missed a conditioning drill, Hoffmann snatched him on the sideline and unleashed a physical beating. As teammates struggled to intervene, defensive coordinator Jim Lambright walked over and called off the Hammer. Lambright told the defensive tackle, "If you miss that drill again, then next time I'll let him finish the job."

When it came to the opponents' rushing attack, the Husky defense excelled at finishing the job. "Shutting down the run was a big deal to me and Emtman," says Hoff. "It was a source of pride. We talked about it a lot. That was our baby. We really felt like we were physically going to rip guys and destroy them. When teams tried running up the middle on us, we couldn't believe our eyes and found it personally offensive. Of course, this meant they had to pay for having the audacity. But as the '91 season wore on, teams saw it was unrealistic to even consider running up the gut.

"Given all the years he spent on the farm with loud equipment, Emtman didn't have the best hearing," says Hoff. "When me and Chico were up there shouting signals, Emtman was on the line facing straight ahead with his earholes not in position to hear us. Oftentimes he couldn't. Sometimes I would have to walk up and give him a hard slap on the ass or reach down and grab his facemask and shout the new signal. I didn't have much time to do that because they could snap the ball at any time. But it was a brotherly way of saying *'Hey this is what we're doing... We're checking to this... Hey I want you to move here!'* Its the inside backer's job to have everyone in the right spots and check to the correct audibles. There can be no mistakes."

After a play where Emtman and/or Hoffmann went nuclear in the opponent's backfield, they always slammed their helmets together and wrapped mammoth arms around each other while shaking violently in celebration. Sweat and blood would be trickling down Hoff's forehead and spilling into his eyes as he roared *GREAT JOB BROTHER!* before swiveling his head in search of other teammates to maul.

"Often times we would both make plays and we weren't even in on the tackle," Hoffmann says. "Maybe Steve destroyed the guard and fullback and freed up someone else to make the tackle, or I happened to blow up the ISO and someone else got to the ball carrier. The crowd may not have noticed it, be we did. When you're down there in the thick of it, you hear that blast of a 90MPH car crash. There's no doubt as to what happened. Steve and I did those things. When you seek and destroy and blow up a play—that fires up everybody on defense!"

Steve Emtman wasn't the only one raising hell on the defensive line; players like D'Marco Farr and Tyrone Rodgers were also punching through. "But what set Steve apart was his ability to single-handedly collapse the pocket," says Hoffmann. "That meant the opposing quarterback was never going to be able to stand there comfortably. Under duress like that, a quarterback's only option besides collapsing into the fetal position was to scramble outside. But good luck to you when you meet Mr. Donald Jones out there. Against our defense there was nowhere to hide. As a matter of fact, most big hits aren't noticed by the fans. When a backer blows up lineman or jackjaws a fullback to bounce the play, only a few people know about it. This is what players mean when they talk about having the respect of their teammates and opponents."

As October played out, each opponent bore witness to the Husky juggernaut. Postgame comments reflected the awe. After the 54-0 win over Arizona, head coach Dick Tomey heaped praise on the Huskies. "Their defense is dominant," he said. "Steve Emtman has to be the best lineman in the country. Nobody blocks him and the folks around him are great football players. Washington is as good a team as the Pac-10 has had, ever."

The following week, the Huskies crushed Toledo 48-0 and their former offensive coordinator Gary Pinkel. "They are an amazingly difficult team to prepare for," said Pinkel, who took over at Toledo after 12 seasons as a Washington assistant. "They are right where they want to be. The best football team in America."

Seven days later, the Huskies faced their toughest test since Nebraska, when they traveled to Strawberry Canyon to face the undefeated and highly ranked California Bears. In the third quarter, the score was tied at 17, as Memorial Stadium ruptured with noise from the sellout crowd and the Berkeley student section jumped up and down and hyperventilated with glee. But Washington took the upper hand when Beno Bryant broke free for a 65-yard touchdown gallop giving the Huskies a 24-17 lead. Late in the fourth quarter, Cal drove to Husky 23 and faced a critical third-and-two. Hoffmann raced through the middle of the line and knocked the ball loose from quarterback Mike Pawlawski, resulting in a 13-yard loss which helped kill the drive. "He's got his mistakes down to almost zero," Don James said of Hoffmann. "There are so many mental things - calls and shifts and judgments. He's done a good job with that." The Huskies toughed out the road win, impressing Cal coach Bruce Snyder in the process. "Against that good a football team, a team that motivated and that skilled, you need to play damn perfect," Snyder said.

October concluded with a home game against the Oregon Ducks, an up-and-coming team that had long fostered a little brother complex toward Washington. The Husky offense didn't fire on all cylinders, but did more than enough in a 29-7 win. The Ducks broke the shutout by scoring a TD in the game's final two minutes against UW reserves— a fact that angered the starters. "I said it before the game that Washington is the best team I've seen in this league ever, and I still stand by that," said longtime Oregon coach Rich Brooks. "I thought we made them work for it. The main problem was we couldn't move the football against them."

Heading into November, Washington had a 7-0 record and the #3 ranking in both national polls, behind Florida State and Miami. But the players' focus remained on the next rung of the ladder, which was a home game against Arizona State. Little did Hoffmann know that a great surprise was in store for him personally. The game itself quickly proved to be a vicious first round knockout and featured the Walter Bailey Show. "Sweet B" was an outstanding cornerback and special-teams contributor. He intercepted a pass on the game's first play from scrimmage and returned it deep into enemy territory. Washington quickly converted it into a touchdown. On the ensuing kickoff, ASU coughed up the ball again and Bailey jumped on it, which led to a second touchdown. Before many in the sellout crowd at Husky Stadium had even sat down, Washington led 14-0. By halftime, the score ballooned to 31-0 and the Huskies had outgained the Sun Devils in yardage 243-40. Into the third quarter, that lead expanded to 41-0.

"We were dominating," recalls Hoffmann. "This was the part

of the game that me and Emtman dreaded. We would start talking about how much longer they were going to let us stay in the game. Two of the assistant coaches, Chris Tormey and Randy Hart, were Lambright's eyes and ears on the sideline. I almost didn't want to look over at them for fear they were going to yank me out of the game. But this time Randy Hart started yelling 'Hoff! Cliff! Get over here!' He grabbed us and shouted: 'Both you guys are going to be in there the next series!'"

Dave Hoffmann and James Clifford locked eyes, smiled and then hugged. It was to be the first time in two years that the duo would play side-by-side in an official game, due to Clifford's knee injury. Moments later they jogged onto the field and huddled with the defense. "Lambright called a Tuff front," Hoffmann says. "That was our version of the aggressive 46 Defense. I was now playing the backer spot which meant I got up on the tight end and loaded up for the 'fight in the phone booth'. The ball was snapped and I fought off a couple blockers and grabbed the ball carrier and pulled him down to the turf. While lying there at the bottom of the pile, I heard the PA announcer say, "...DAVE HOFFMANN AND JAMES CLIFFORD ON THE TACKLE." I looked over and Cliffy was laying on the turf too, looking over at me. We just smiled. We were like, *Yeah, that's right!*

"Once we got to our feet, we reached out over the top of the running back and high-fived each other," Hoffmann says. "A picture of that moment appeared in the next day's Seattle Times. I loved playing with Chico as much as anybody in my whole career, but it was great to be out there with my best friend James Clifford. How awesome that on the first play we combine for a tackle for loss."

After that series finished, the defense came off the field with the 41-0 lead intact. The UW coaches announced they were yanking starters. "I kicked over a folding chair and had words with coach Tormey," Hoffmann says. "I felt like it was too early, and that happened in a lot of our games. Getting the chance to play was my form of pay. Just because we're kicking the living snot out of the other team, don't take away my great time and my joy. Just because we're doing our job at such a supreme level, don't punish us for that. That was my attitude and I let it be known. That happened a lot in 1991. There were times we would go in at halftime and the coaches would tell us we would get one series in the third quarter before giving way to the backups. And you had to swallow it. I'm not saying it was right or wrong, but we had earned the opportunity to have played a little longer. Don't get me wrong, we had guys like Steve Springstead and Hillary Butler that were great young linebackers that needed to get out there. But a couple more series in each game would have meant a lot to us.

"I never gave thought to what the final scores would have been had the starters played entire games," Hoff says. "But when we watched film in the team room the coaches would tell us we were #1 in the nation in rushing defense at 65 yards per game. And I would pipe up and say, 'HEY, if you KEEP US IN LONGER we could be holding opponents to under 20 YARDS RUSHING A GAME... LET'S DO IT!' I definitely wish we could have played longer in so many of those games, and I am speaking not just for me and Emtman, but all the guys. A lot of that didn't make sense. But at the same time, it was the first time the Huskies had experienced such dominance in its history. Even with all the great Husky teams of the past, none dominated like our teams did. We blew other teams right out of the stadium in the first half."

CHAPTER 13

WITH NEWS THAT FLORIDA STATE fell to Miami, the Huskies moved up to the #2 spot in the national ranking to go along with their 8-0 record. Up next: The USC Trojans in the Los Angeles Coliseum. One year had passed since the 31-0 thrashing in Seattle. Quarterback Todd Marinovich had bolted early for the NFL, but remaining Trojans were talking revenge. It was sure to be an intense battle. Dave Hoffmann's fondest memories of that week revolve around the late Jaime Fields (1970-1999).

"Jaime played linebacker alongside me and was somebody I respected and liked from the first day we met," Hoff says. "He was just real. We had lots of good talks about family, faith and football. He was from Compton, California. When we were both homesick freshmen we counted down the days before we could head down to Thanksgiving. Returning to Los Angeles to play USC in front of family and friends got Jaime very excited. We talked about it several times that week."

"The most intimidating member of Washington's defense was weakside linebacker Jaime Fields, whose light blue, wolf like eyes played off his coffee skin," wrote Sam Farmer in the book *Bitter Roses*. "He was listed in the press guide at 6 feet, but his compact 230-pound frame made him appear an inch or two shorter. The thick knot of muscles in his upper back almost reached his earlobes, giving him the look of a snarling pit bull."

"Jaime laid shots on guys and he always had my back and I had his," Hoff says. "He was always in on the action. Playing side-by-side as the weak side/outside linebacker, he was right next to me. We worked together with communicating as far as changing assignments as we were checking our calls, or if we were going into a combo coverage and going to be teaming up on guys in man-to-man coverage. By the time we were juniors in 1991, our communication had become finely honed. All we needed was to give each other a look and a nod. We knew what the other was thinking. It was a really good feeling."

The media reminded everyone all week about how Washington hadn't won at the Los Angeles Coliseum since 1980, but most Husky players weren't mindful of the chirping. As they boarded the plane, Hoffmann and Fields talked about wreaking havoc and doing big things. "Some people talk about playing a 'bend but don't break' defense," says Hoffmann. "But we weren't even going to bend. We had made up our minds to fully impose our will on USC's offense."

Coming out of the tunnel, Dave and Jaime were fired up and gave each other a piece of their helmets. Once out onto the Coliseum's grass surface and amid the heat, they got after it. "USC has always been known for being physical but we had become the Kings of the Pac-10," Hoff says. "It was good to let them know again what the pecking order was. We were reminding USC who carried the bigger stick. We were tuning guys up!"

It would be a low-scoring affair. UW struck first when Beno Bryant took a deep handoff from Billy Joe Hobert, found a hole at right tackle, cut to his left and sprinted untouched up the middle for a 55-yard touchdown. In the second quarter, Washington's lead expanded to 14-0 when Bryant scored again on a seven-yard run.

That was the end of UW's scoring. Bryant had a big day with 158 yards rushing, but the offense struggled to get on track. By late in the fourth quarter, Washington led 14-3. "I know that score wasn't impressive, but their offense couldn't move the ball on us and we were bringing it," Hoffmann says. "I was having a good day. I made a tackle for loss when USC threw a swing pass on fourth down—and I really blasted the guy and drove him into the turf. On another play I sacked quarterback Reggie Perry at the USC 1-yard line. Still another time, I pursued a toss sweep play and wrapped up the running back and twisted his head as I dragged him to the ground.

"Jaime and I had been unloading on their fullbacks, linemen and tight ends all game long. I remember just looking over at him. When you play together that long with someone you almost don't have to speak at times, you could just look at each other and know what the other guy was thinking. Late in the game, USC tried a running play on third down and short. Jaime and I just engulfed it. We hammered the full back and blasted the ball carrier for a tackle for loss. We were high-fiving and jumping up and down like we always did, running off the field. We plopped down on the bench together, talking about the play we had just made. Jaime and I couldn't stop laughing because we had been absolutely destroying their fullback who previously thought he was the cock of the walk. It was just the joy and excitement. We were only up by 11, so it wasn't like we were blowing them out of the water like the previous year. But we knew that USC couldn't move the ball on us. We were just having fun and enjoying life together. I mean, that was living! There was nothing more enjoyable than to be out there together playing the game of football and doing well. We were just in the moment together.

"So Jaime and I are over there laughing like a couple of kids, and assistant coach Randy Hart, whom I have a good relationship with, comes over to us with his headset on. He screams, HOFFMANN! FIELDS! GET THOSE SMILES OFF YOUR FACES! CAN'T YOU SEE THE SCOREBOARD? THERE'S STILL TWO MINUTES LEFT! THIS THING ISN'T OVER! Well, Jaime and I started laughing with everything we had. Coach Hart gave me a look, and then slapped me in the face. Jaime and I stopped and looked at each other, then started laughing even harder. And I reached up and slapped Coach Hart, and knocked his headset off!

"Coach Hart shook his head and walked away. He knew we had our heads in the game and that the defense had control of things. But he was just doing what a good coach does and playing the part. He sees a couple of guys acting crazy on the sideline and he came over just to keep them in line."

When the clock ran out, Washington had beaten USC for the second year in a row. The Dawgs improved their record to 9-0 and needed one more win to clinch a second straight trip to the Rose Bowl. Afterwards, friends and family waited outside the LA Coliseum as the players emerged on their way to the team busses. Dave's little brother Matt was wearing a Husky jersey with HOFFMANN on the back. All of sudden behind him he hears a big voice shout "HEY FIFTY-FOUR!" He turned to look and it was Dick Butkus, the Pro Football Hall of Fame linebacker. Butkus now had a son on USC's team and was waiting for him. He shouted, "Tell your brother NICE GAME!"

On the plane ride back home, Dave and Jaime celebrated Jaime's victorious homecoming with high-fives and smiles. Little did either of them know that eight years later Jaime would be killed in a hit-and-run collision when a driver T-boned his car at a California intersection.

"To this day, I think about Jaime all the time," Dave says.

CHAPTER 14

ON A RAINY NOVEMBER night in Corvallis, Oregon, the Washington Huskies captured their second straight Rose Bowl berth by whipping Oregon State 58-6. Grandma and Grandpa Hoffmann were out that way for a speaking engagement and had attended the game. Grandpa Ozzie was a long-time speaker of The Lutheran Hour radio show. He always told his grandson, "Dave, remember to love Jesus and have a sense of humor!" After the game, Dave sat in the locker room pulling thorns off the rose he had been given, knowing he was going to give it to his grandma. "It was okay for her grandson to have a bloody forehead but not for her to have bloody fingers," he says. As I gave it to her outside the locker room, she said, 'My oh my, thank you so much Dave,' and then gave me a kiss."

The regular season concluded one week later under gray skies at Husky Stadium. Washington wrapped up a perfect regular season with a 56-21 win over the Cougs. It was UW's first perfect record since the days of legendary coach Gil Dobie in 1916. "We had a great time coming after their quarterback Drew Bledsoe," Hoff says. "You could tell he was going to be a special quarterback, but we had our way that day. We were headed back to the Rose Bowl. Our celebration was happy but kept in perspective. We had one final rung on the ladder to climb."

In the week leading up to New Year's Day, local and national media both touted the dream matchup at hand: #2 Washington with an 11-0 record against #4 Michigan at 9-1-1. A crowd of over 105,000 was expected at the Rose Bowl in addition to millions of viewers around the world. As Hoffmann lifted weights and went through drills, he envisioned wreaking destruction on college football's biggest stage.

History was at stake. On a late December night, Huskies Ed Cunningham, James Clifford and Brett Collins were having dinner with Cunningham's family at an Anaheim restaurant. An older guy got up from his chair and strode over to their table. Never identifying himself, he stuck out his oversized fist and displayed a 1966 national championship ring from Notre Dame. He told them, "This is what's it all about. Win this one, and you can live with it the rest of your lives!"

Cunningham said it helped frame the historical significance for him, but Hoff didn't need any further motivation. He felt prepared from all the hard work during those dark rainy nights that Dan Lloyd told him about.

Meanwhile, Michigan's roster was a treasure trove of future NFL talent. Legendary ABC broadcaster Keith Jackson said the Wolverines possessed the best offensive line he'd ever seen. Michigan also boasted quarterback Elvis Grbac and wide receiver Desmond Howard, the winner of that year's Heisman Trophy. "But the way our coaches prepared us, I felt like I was inside the mind of the other team's offensive coordinator," Hoffmann says. "Lambright was already way in there. I felt like Lambright walked into the mind of our opponent's coordinator. This was the way we prepared every week."

Former UW center Ed Cunningham delights in a certain memory. "By that stage of the season, our practices were so finely tuned," Cunningham said. "But when you get to bowl practice, there's a little more time to do some real hard technique work and go back to training camp a little bit. I remember the defense just looked different. They were doing something different. They were doing a lot of adjustments early on in their preparation. At dinner one night, I was talking with Dave. I said 'Dave, what's going on?' He said 'Man, I'm not sure how we're doing it, but we're going to have about three sets of eyeballs on Desmond Howard on every play. I kind of feel sorry for him.'"

"Yes, I said that," Hoffmann says. "Not out of arrogance, but matter-of-factly out of belief in the thoroughness of our preparation. To Michigan's credit, they had great players and good guys. A quality football team. But I just felt that with our talent, attitude and preparation we were going to lay it to them."

As fans filled the Rose Bowl's enormous sprawl on this sun-drenched New Year's Day, Hoff and his teammates stood upon the immaculate turf for warm-ups. During butt drills, The Hitman was laying his usual massive shots on teammates, then clapping his hands in excitement as he got back in line to await his next turn. His golden Husky helmet gleamed in the mid-day glare, digging repeatedly into his forehead from the battering barrage, as sweat and blood spilled into his eyes and trickled down his nose.

Team chaplain Mike Rohrbach stood nearby and watched with a smile of his own. "Being an old linebacker, I would hang out with the linebackers in pre-game warm ups," Rorhbach said. "Sometimes I would think, 'Oh my gosh, I hope we have something left in the tank for the game because these guys are flat out beating the snot out of each other.' I would shout, HEY HOFF, TAKE IT EASY BUDDY! He would just look at you and snort."

At about 2PM, as Hoffmann ran with his teammates out onto the field in front of 105,366 fans and saw Michigan across the way, he knew this was it. In his physical prime at 6'2" and 230 pounds, the coiled, violent spring of his body had been tightened and retightened from years of training and visualization. Husky fans filled one half of the stadium, Wolverine fans the other. Electricity pulsated in the air. Back in the state of Washington, people gathered around TV sets with sweaty palms. It was later announced that in the Nielsen overnight ratings that 75% of households in Western Washington were tuned into the game. Across America, 1 in 4 homes were watching.

Michigan kicked off and UW's freshman sensation Napoleon Kaufman caught it and accelerated up field, zipping past defenders and crossing midfield before being tripped up by a shoestring. Teammate Leif Johnson lifted him high in the air as teammates celebrated on their way back to the sideline. But Washington's opening drive quickly stalled and the Huskies were forced to punt.

So Elvis Grbac and Desmond Howard led their offense onto the field for their initial crack at the Husky defense. Hoff leaned into the huddle and shouted out the call before scurrying to line up as Michigan's mammoth offensive line approached. In that quiet moment, Hoff took control of his emotions to think quickly and clearly as a surgeon at the operating table. "When Michigan got the ball for their first possession, they ran an ISO off tackle, like they were testing our manhood," Hoffmann says. "I blasted the fullback and made the tackle. Our weeks of preparation enabled us to take little cheats to angle toward their tendencies. As the game wore on, we were making tackles for no gain or tackles for losses. It felt familiar. It felt good. We were throttling their offense."

By halftime the Huskies led 14-7, but Hoffmann could sense the tipping point coming. The point where an opponent's psyche breaks and the onslaught ensues. "I felt like we just needed to keep pounding them," he says. "Defensively we came after them like sharks going after meat. I looked into the facemasks of the Michigan players and I saw the looks of confusion. In the second half we started to pull away and there was a feeling of inevitability to it."

Washington's tight ends figured prominently, as Billy Joe Hobert first hit Aaron Pierce for a TD pass and then later connected with Mark Bruner, who used great balance on his tippy toes to stay in bounds in the back of the end zone. This put the Huskies up 27-7 late in the third quarter.

At one point, Michigan began a series in the shadow of their own goal line. On national TV, broadcaster Keith Jackson remarked with disbelief how Washington had shut down Michigan's powerful offense. "This is the best offensive line I've ever seen," Jackson said.

"And Washington has completely dominated them." No sooner were those words uttered then did Steve Emtman bull rush his blocker right into the Michigan running back, knocking him down for a loss. "Folks, that's one of the best offensive lineman in the country and that guy right there just manhandled him." The pass rush proved to be just as relentless. Michigan had only surrendered six quarterback sacks all season long, but the Huskies sacked Grbac six times in the Rose Bowl and knocked him down many other times.

Dusk descended upon the Rose Bowl as the glare of the overhead lights took a glowing effect on the field. Heisman trophy winner Desmond Howard only had one catch and Grbac grew frustrated trying to get him the ball. So the Michigan quarterback tried for his tight end coming across the middle, but only to see him lit up by Hoffmann. Soon after, Grbac dropped back and threw toward wide receiver Jesse Johnson.

"Jaime Fields and I were working a combo coverage," says Hoffmann. "I screamed 'HE'S COMING TO YOU! HE'S COMING TO YOU!' Jaime completely blew him up." As Johnson crumpled to the turf, an awestruck gasp rolled through the stadium followed by cheers from Husky fans.

Moments later, the Husky defense stuffed Grbac's attempted sneak on fourth down. Possession went to Washington, and Mark Brunell entered the game at quarterback. A large brace securing his knee symbolized his long climb back over the past eight months. Upon taking his first snap of the day, he dropped back deep into the pocket, set his feet, and lobbed a throw toward Mario Bailey in the end zone. Bailey made a circus catch for the 38-yard touchdown strike., then jumped to his feet and faced. the Michigan sideline to strike the Heisman pose. Following the extra point, the Huskies were now up 34-7.

Don James and assistant coach Randy Hart signaled for the defensive backups. Michigan's Tyrone Wheatley took advantage, breaking loose for a 53-yard scoring run, to make the final score 34-14. "Deep down a bunch of us wished that we could have left the starters in longer and make the score more lopsided," Hoffmann said. "To show the country just how good we were. But Coach James knew what he was doing and we respected his decision. Everyone on that team deserved to play in that game. No matter what unit they were on, everybody on that team had put in so much work that season."

The clock emptied to 0:00 and Don James jogged to midfield to shake hands with Michigan coach Gary Moeller, who afterwards told the media "I can't envision a better team than Washington." The side of the stadium containing Washington fans sounded out the thunderous chant of "WE'RE NUMBER ONE!... WE'RE NUMBER ONE!" The Husky Marching Band began playing "Tequila!" over and over. "I was out there with all the guys," says Hoff. "I remember hugging my brother, Todd Bridge, James Clifford, Donald Jones, Steve Emtman and many others. I leaned back and screamed, just letting loose. It was a yell of thankfulness and appreciation. We had gotten to the top of the mountain. When you're close to the top you don't want to acknowledge it. But when you get to the peak and the mission is accomplished, you want to let loose. Our season was over. We had reached the final rung of the ladder. We had gone 12-0."

Following the locker room celebration, post-game interviews and hoopla, it was over. Hoff sat quietly with his family at a restaurant enjoying a meal. Upon returning to his hotel room, he set his duffel bag on the floor. It was a little heftier than usual. Back in the locker room Hoff had remembered what happened the year before and now felt no qualms about slipping his helmet into his bag.

"Even though I was tired and wiped out, it was important to walk around the hotel and see all the guys," Hoffmann says. "To give them a hug and shoot the bull." The hotel was set up as a square, and the Huskies occupied an entire floor. Players, coaches and family members could do a loop and visit with the entire team. At that moment, in Florida's Orange Bowl, top-ranked Miami played Nebraska. "I wasn't keeping an eye on the TV," Hoffmann says. "I'm sure I asked what the score was but it wasn't a priority for me that evening. The priority was this special group of guys that had achieved perfection."

Washington's 12-0 record was the first perfect season in the Pac-10 since the 1972 USC Trojans accomplished the feat. Relaxing that evening, players began to reflect.

"I'm around the game a lot and it's been a big part of my life and will continue to be for many years," said Ed Cunningham, former Husky captain and current ABC broadcaster. "Every now and then there's just a season where something magical happens with a team. It's a tapestry where all the pieces got sewn together in the right order. Where they're all different coming from different places and with different styles. A guy like Dave Hoffmann, he looks like a spike. Because his neck and shoulders are four feet across and when you follow the line down to his ankles it's a pin. How does a guy like that become an All-American? Well, he's a good guy with an amazing work ethic, knows how to read defenses, wants to see the team succeed, and oh by the way, he hits *really hard*. You find all these weird tapestry pieces that come together. These pieces are athletic enough and coached well enough to win at the highest level. And secondly, there's that X factor that if you knew what it was you would be a billionaire. It's that elusive chemistry. It creates a team tapestry so strong and so well sewn together that there's no way that it's coming apart during an entire football season."

As it happened, Miami went on to beat Nebraska 22-0 and also finished 12-0. Voting to determine the national champion was underway and would be announced the next morning. It proved to be a split vote and a shared national title. The Associated Press sided with the Hurricanes, while the USA Today/CNN poll gave the Huskies the nod. In Newsday, writer Bob Glauber wrote: "America, say hello to the Washington Huskies. Tucked away all this time in the nation's upper left-hand corner, seemingly three time zones from college football civilization, the No. 2 Huskies finally took center stage at the time that mattered most."

"There was no BCS Championship game in those days," says Hoffmann. "People have asked me many times since what would have happened had Washington played Miami. If we had played Miami we would have beaten them. They had a great team with plenty of speed and talent. But overall, with our linemen and offense and front seven on defense, we would have beat them up physically. I'm not saying it would have been a cakewalk, but we would have worn them down as the game went on. If we had played them three times we would have beaten them three times."

After a few days off, the players returned to Seattle for the start of winter quarter. The team and fans alike wondered what sort of parade or civic party would commemorate the national championship. As time went on, however, it became clear from athletic director Barbara Hedges that none would be forthcoming.

"I was kind of disappointed that Barbara Hedges didn't want to have a parade or celebration," said linebacker Donald Jones. "I was part of a small committee that met with her. She didn't want to deal with the hassle of putting it together. But it was disappointing because it was history in the making. We wanted a chance to celebrate with the fans and students and the people of Seattle. Life is short, man. We don't get a chance to celebrate moments like that very often."

"We may have been disappointed," says Hoffmann, "but we were a bunch of hard-working warriors who were humble so we weren't ones to sit around complaining about not having a parade. My thoughts turned to guys who weren't going to be there anymore. Guys like Donald Jones, Chico Fraley and Dana Hall."

Soon to be added to this list was Steve Emtman, who announced in January that he was forgoing his senior season to apply for the 1992 NFL Draft.

CHAPTER 15

PRIOR TO THE 1992 NFL Draft, no Husky football player had ever gone higher in the first round than the seventh spot, where Reggie Rogers was selected by the Detroit Lions in 1987. When the Indianapolis Colts selected Steve Emtman with the first overall pick in the 1992 NFL Draft, everyone associated with Husky Football smiled and high-fived at the historical significance. Hoffmann and many players piled into cars and drove over to the home of teammate Bruce Bailey's parents in the luxurious neighborhood of Laurelhurst. "We had a big breakfast and then the TV stations came out to interview Steve," Hoffmann says. "I remember standing up on the porch and watching ESPN interview Steve's mom and dad. His dad is an eastern Washington farmer, and he was so excited. He had his arm around Mrs. Emtman and was slapping and clubbing her back. I nudged my brother and said, 'Look! Mr. Emtman is going to hurt her!' But Mrs. Emtman was so tough and remained unfazed. They were so excited."

Emtman had won the Lombardi Award and Outland Trophy, as well as being named the Pac-10 Defensive Player of the Year for the second consecutive season. He now had the nation's eyes upon him and a nice payday in front of him. Hoffmann chuckled in recalling the times he and Emtman lived together in a rental house in Lake City, that they called 'The Country Club'. "We had to put foil and plastic wrap around the windows to try to keep the heat in during the winters," Hoff says. "In retrospect it probably kept the cold in more than anything."

Emtman and the seniors were gone, but thoughts of the upcoming '92 season sent the remaining Huskies straight back into the weight room. James Clifford's knee supported him in cutting and planting, and optimism abounded for him. He and Dave were going to play alongside each other extensively for the first time since 1989. In addition, Dave's brother Steve was entering his redshirt freshman year, and would be eligible to play.

During spring ball, Don James stood before the team and announced it was time to elect senior captains. Two for offense and two for defense. Assistants passed scratches of paper throughout the team room. Everyone scribbled down their choice before tossing it into the ballot box.

"I felt honored to be elected captain for my senior year," Hoffmann says. "But the biggest thing about being captain is that the guys who are leaders already feel like they're leaders. It's an unspoken thing. I don't even know how you know. Even if you're on scout team you know you're a leader. But you don't want to be yappin' all the time like one of those mother hens and annoying SOBs. It's more important to lead by example. We had lots of guys leading by example. We had guys that were such warriors that we didn't care for the rah-rah stuff, which suited me fine. But the players voted and that was the most important thing to me. It was most meaningful to be elected by them, and not by somebody that wasn't with me in the trenches."

Joining Hoffmann as captains were Lincoln Kennedy, Shane Pahukoa and Mark Brunell. The pieces were now in place for another run. The Washington Huskies were on a mission to become the first team in history to ever win three straight Rose Bowls.

That mission began officially in fall camp, August 1992. Dave roomed with brother Steve. In the old Crew House, each room had bunk beds. Dave and Steve used the upper bunk for storage so they took the mattress off of it and placed it on the floor. On a nearby table sat a copy of the *Guinness Book of World Records,* which Mrs.

Hoffmann had given to her boys as a Christmas gift. Each night after exhausting themselves in fall camp drills and scrimmages, the brothers returned to the room looking forward to an evening of rest. "I would grab that book and open it up," Dave says. "For fun, I would read aloud some obscure record and challenge Steve to guess within forty pounds the weight of the largest watermelon of all time, or whatever. If he got it right he got to choose whether he got the bed or the floor. We would be so achy and tired but it was funny to try to guess some stupid record to determine who got to sleep in which spot. Little details like that made that time together special."

The season opened September 5th on a sweltering night in the Arizona desert. "I appreciated running out of the tunnel with my brother," Dave says. "It was special and we knew it. Playing at night in the warm air on the grass was always a blast. I always loved putting on the black hat and going into the enemy's backyard."

Arizona State nourished a reputation as a party school teeming with beautiful co-eds. A chain link fence right behind the opposing team's bench enabled fans to linger within close range. ASU recruited gorgeous girls with bronzed skin, dazzling smiles, and intoxicating perfume, and positioned them right behind the Washington bench. "I warned the guys not to be distracted by the pretty girls," Hoff says. "I was saying this mostly for the benefit of the young guys who hadn't been down there before. I wanted to remind them that while we were red-blooded American males we were also on a business trip and we needed to stay focused on being dominant."

The Huskies had a new look this season. Napoleon Kaufman would get more time at running back along with Beno Bryant. Jamal Fountaine became a starter at linebacker and D'Marco Farr took over Emtman's spot at defensive tackle. Billy Joe Hobert and Mark Brunell would continue to split time at quarterback. Defensively the Huskies were as aggressive as ever.

"One of our calls would shift the defensive front," Hoffmann says. "Sometimes I would yell MOVE! and our linemen would shift in unison either to the left or the right. This was to confuse the other team's offensive linemen about who they were supposed to block. Against ASU, on the first third and short, I made the call just before the snap to get them to jump. The quarterback called out signals… 'Down.. Set…' and then I yelled MOVE! MOVE! MOVE! before he said 'Hike'. ASU players were jumping early and flags were flying. They were getting backed up five yards a pop. I did it three or four times, just having fun with it. I couldn't believe how easy it was to draw their guys offside. There was a pause in the action and Don James hollered at me. I ran over to the sideline. He told me with a bit stronger language, 'Dave, knock it off, will ya? We're going to be here all night!' I said, 'yes sir,' and ran back out to the huddle.

"One of my all-time favorite moments came from that game," said former UW team chaplain Mike Rohrbach. "The ASU running back came out of the backfield and Hoff hit the guy. I call it the *Rattlesnake Strike*. Hoff hit the guy and the guy went backwards and down on the ground and Hoff was just standing there, reminiscent of the old Ray Nitschke picture with the Green Bay Packers, where he stood over him frothing at the mouth. Hoff just totally took the guy out. It happened in a split second."

Washington won the game 31-7. The Huskies did surrender 214 yards rushing to Mario Bates, but overall kept the Sun Devil offense in check. Offensively, UW's Napoleon Kaufman created shockwaves. Despite only carrying the ball six times, he gained 159 yards and scored a touchdown. In the next day's Seattle Times, the headline was NAPOLEON MARCHES ON TEMPE.

The Huskies returned home the next week to Husky Stadium and beat Wisconsin 27-10. Some regarded it a ragged performance. But they had beaten a Big 10 opponent, were 2-0, ranked #2 in the nation and had won 14 games in a row dating back to 1990. With the powerhouse Nebraska Cornhuskers coming to town for a rematch, the nation's focus would be trained upon Seattle.

CHAPTER 16

IN COLLEGE FOOTBALL, ANTICIPATION for a game can be every bit as delicious as the contest itself. With the Washington Huskies now among the nation's elite, the mere idea of powerhouse Nebraska coming to town had the Pacific Northwest abuzz. Sportswriters from all across the country secured media passes and made their way to Seattle to cram the press boxes. Sports radio shows fielded calls from hyperventilating callers. Legions of fans wore purple all week leading up to the game. Extra lights were erected at Husky Stadium, as ESPN would be televising the game nationally—only the second night game there in its history.

"Last season we had gone into their back yard and taken their candy," says Hoffmann. "This time around, they were coming to Seattle to try to take it back. Nobody on our team had played a night game at Husky Stadium before. Best of all, it was still September, so the evening weather would be warm. I was fired up. The whole team was. We wanted to show Nebraska and the entire nation that last year wasn't a fluke and that we were still the best."

"It was one of those nights to remember," recalled former Husky All-American Lincoln Kennedy. "Because when you came into the stadium, the air was so thick with anticipation, it was almost jubilation. You really had trouble containing yourself. The late afternoon sky had pigments of orange and pink to it, and as it grew dark, the night was so clear. You actually felt like you could do no wrong. Those kinds of moments in life don't come along very often."

From the opening kickoff, the crowd of 73,333 generated a blast furnace of noise and energy. "We were going to have fun and get after it," Hoff says. "On Nebraska's first play from scrimmage, I made sure to really stroke the center—to hit him so hard that the back of his helmet touched the back of his shoulder pads. To really send them the message that they had better get ready for another physical beating."

After a scoreless first quarter, Washington's John Werdel pinned Nebraska deep inside their 5-yard line with a great punt. On first down Nebraska ran the fullback dive; Hoffmann shot the hole and tackled the ball carrier inside the one yard line. After a false start penalty, Nebraska broke huddle from their end zone and approached the line of scrimmage. The bloodthirsty crowd was in a froth. The Huskies lined up in their Tuff formation, with nine players crowding the line of scrimmage. Hoffmann had made a Rover Dog call, which would send a safety and linebacker on a blitz on the tight end side. Safety Tommie Smith roared in unchallenged toward Nebraska quarterback Mike Gant's blindside. Every set of eyes in the crowd could see the impending car crash, save for Gant, who simply tried to set his feet for a pass. At the precise moment of impact, Gant's body was drilled into the end zone turf, as ESPN sideline crews measured the noise at 133.6 decibels; one of the loudest moments in college football history. The Husky defense celebrated all the way to the bench with a 2-0 lead.

Late in the second quarter Washington was leading 9-7, when the Huskies scored two touchdowns in the span of 42 seconds. Napoleon Kaufman had a long run down the left side that got the offense deep into Cornhusker territory. Moments later Kaufman scored on a short dive, putting UW ahead 16-7. On Nebraska's ensuing drive, Walter "Sweet B" Bailey picked off a Gant pass right along the sideline. Billy Joe Hobert promptly connected with Joe Kralik for a 29-yard touchdown pass. That score put Washington up 23-7 at halftime.

The Cornhuskers scored a touchdown early in the third quarter to close the gap to 23-14, but that would be as close things would get on the scoreboard. But that didn't mean personal scores weren't being settled on the field.

"At one point Nebraska ran a screen play to my left hand side," Hoffmann says. "I had seen on film that their linemen would come down field and chop block on screen plays. So I ran out to make the play as two blockers were gunning for me. I played one blocker with my hands as I thought he was going to chop me low. I didn't give him the normal shot that I usually would. I was occupied with steering the play back inside. After the play, the Nebraska guy said, 'MAN HOFFMANN, I THOUGHT YOU WERE SUPPOSED TO BE THE SHIT!' I just nodded and smiled and said, 'You just worry about yourself.' As he walked back to his huddle, I made note of his jersey number.

"A couple plays later, the play went off to my right. Our guys had it enveloped for a sure tackle for loss. I spotted that guy off to my left. I don't normally do this kind of thing, but I made off like a laser beam right for his ear. I absolutely blasted him. He felt it, man. He looked up at me like he wasn't quite sure what city he was in. I gave him a big smile and went back to celebrate with my teammates."

Washington won the game 29-14 to improve to 3-0 overall. The next week, as the players entered the team room to break down game film, Hoffmann was curious to Lambright's reaction to his deviation from the game plan.

"When we were watching film the next week, that play came up on the screen in the team room," Hoffmann says. "All my teammates go running off to the right to make the play, while I took two steps and then WHOOM! I go flying out of the picture in the opposite direction. I was ready to explain myself, but Lambright never said anything. We had been around each other long enough that he knew if I was doing something like that I had a good reason for it. I was just taking care of some personal business. Needless to say, I made sure we had the play secured before I would go off and do something like that.

"That's exactly what you love about Dave and why he was great at what he was doing," said Lambright. "After I had been coaching him for awhile, the last thing I was going to do was question something like that or run the film back."

CHAPTER 17

WASHINGTON FOLLOWED UP THE win over Nebraska with a 17-10 win over USC that left the Huskies at 4-0 and now ranked #1 in the nation, with Miami right on their heels. Now it was the morning of October 10th, and the team exited their Bellevue hotel and filed into the two team busses that were bound for Husky Stadium. A home game against the Cal Bears was a few hours away. In an interesting twist, Cal had a first-year coach—UW's former offensive coordinator Keith Gilbertson.

"Surrounding me on the bus ride was the usual cast characters," Hoffmann says. "My brother Steve, Cliff and Mike Rohrbach. We would save each other seats just like little kids on a school bus."

When the team busses reached Husky Stadium, the players departed their began our pre-game preparations. A couple hours later they ran out onto the field before an electrified crowd and got ready to kickoff. It was strange for them seeing Gilbertson on opponent's sideline. The media touted the game as a showdown between star tailbacks Russell White of Cal vs. Washington's Napoleon Kaufman. White was being hyped as frontrunner in the Heisman Trophy race. But as the game got underway, the Husky defense shut him down while Kaufman ran wild. The Huskies won 35-16, holding White to 35 yards rushing, compared to Kaufman's 216. However, what made the day memorable for Hoffmann was what happened in the second quarter.

"Cal ran a play and I got a good read on the ball," Hoff says. I snapped the guard, hit him hard and threw him off to my right. I penetrated the backfield and tackled the ball carrier. I was wrenching him and holding him up so my teammates could come get a piece. Suddenly I felt someone dive on the back of my legs. It was the blocker I had just beaten on the play. This was a cheap shot in my book. Excruciating pain shot through my left foot. It took me a few seconds to get up. I was sure it was broken. I looked at the clock and saw there wasn't much time before the half would be over. I could walk but I was in agony. Tears ran down my face. I was near the Cal sideline. Coach Gilbertson must have seen my grimace. He shouted, HOFF, ARE YOU OKAY? When I didn't respond, he yelled it again. I tried to give him a nod but my mind raced with questions: How much time would I miss? How long would I be out? How was this going to affect my career?"

Halftime arrived and Dave managed to get up the tunnel by leaning on Mike Rohrbach for support to help take weight off the foot. "I was leaning on him not just physically but emotionally as well. I went straight for the training room. It looked like a possible fracture but mainly it was a horrible sprain. You could see the black mark in the x-ray, where basically my foot had been bent in half the long way, like a hot dog bun. The training staff said it wasn't broken, or at least not badly, and that it was ultimately my call. I asked them to tape it up with a little something extra. They put a super tight wrap job on it.

"I leaned on Mike Rohrbach all the way back down the tunnel for the second half," Dave says. "I tried to go out and do some slow back peddles and some side-to-sides to make sure I could push on the foot. I knew that I could stay upright on my own two feet but wouldn't be able to plant on it like normal. But I was going to be able to compete. Moments before the start of the second half, I was seated among the folding chairs grabbing a sip of Gatorade. Rohrbach came over and put his hand on the back of my neck and prayed aloud for me. With Rohr, he wouldn't have had to ask for permission for something like that from me. I appreciated it. I needed everything I could get right there."

During the second half, as Washington pulled away, the coaches pulled the starters. It was the only time in Hoffmann's life that he was relieved to be removed from a game. For the following week, and the rest of the season, he walked around campus in a therapeutic boot with a Velcro strap. "I would practice as much as I could, stay off it as much as I could, and then play on Saturdays," Hoff says. "That proved to be one of those injuries that never leave you. To this day it can flare up under too much physical stress.

The convincing win over Cal ran Washington's record to 5-0 and the Associated Press voted them #1 in the nation. A road trip to hostile Eugene drew near. On Friday night the Huskies had their usual short practice and run around on the opponent's field to get acclimated. "Don James never had us wear practice jerseys, but just t-shirts that said Washington Huskies on them," Hoff says. "It made it harder for any spies from the opposing teams to pick us out. Coach James asked me to go hide out in the tunnel area so it wouldn't be obvious that I had an injury. You don't want to broadcast who's hurt and what you're doing."

The next day the Dawgs got suited up and went out for pre-game warm-ups. The energized crowd that was rapidly filling the stadium rained boos down upon them. It was ingrained in the DNA of every Duck fan to hate Washington. The fact the Huskies were the nation's #1 team only served to amplify their bloodlust. At Autzen Stadium, fans are virtually right on top of the field and can give opponents an earful. Sure enough, as the Husky linebackers began warming up in the end zone, the raucous Oregon student section started in on the obscenities. Enduring the pain in his foot, Hoff's scowl told teammates he was digging deep. The grunts and smacks of shoulder pads sounded out with each successive collision as the Dawgs went through their drills. Suddenly, a Duck fan stood up and shouted "YOU GUYS AREN'T DAWGS! YOU'RE DOG SHIT!" He made a throwing motion, and suddenly a dog biscuit skittered across the turf and came to rest at defensive coordinator Jim Lambright's feet.

"We're warming up, right down from their student section," Lambright recalled. "We're going through our butt drills, strike press and release drills, and some tackling drills. All of a sudden somebody was throwing dog biscuits at us. I picked one up and started to talk to the linebackers about my thoughts on that. Dave grabbed it out of my hand and pulled off his helmet, turned toward the crowd and ate it. The Oregon fans fell silent in disbelief. Moments later, it became entertainment, as there was a lot of pointing it out and laughter. It was sure one of the funniest damn things I've ever seen. After that, nothing more needed to be said. Everything that needed to be said was taken care of by Dave's actions."

"I never did it for anybody else, just for our little group of linebackers," Hoffmann says. "It was just something I did. We went back to our warm-ups. I think it was my teammate D'Marco Farr that yapped about it to the media after the game. It wasn't a big deal to me and my teammates. But the story took on a little life of its own. Just like with fishing stories, it gets a little bigger as time goes on."

Once the game got underway, Mark Brunell was the starting quarterback for the first time in nearly two years. Don James thought a change was needed as Billy Joe had been struggling with accuracy and confidence. Brunell played a decent game, but defense was the key to victory. Washington got four turnovers—two fumble recoveries and two pass interceptions by cornerback Josh Moore. Oregon quarterback Danny O'Neil ran for his life throughout the game. The final score was Washington 24, Oregon 3.

After the game, Oregon's radio announcers stated these weren't the same Huskies as the year before. "We didn't ever go around comparing ourselves to the year before," Hoffmann says. "We didn't have time to do so even if we wanted. That being said, the 1991 team had lots of great players on defense that were no longer there. Guys like Steve Emtman, Dana Hall, Donald Jones, Chico Fraley and Tyrone Rodgers. That made a difference I'm sure. But we were into our third year of having a lot of success. Talk about becoming a target. Opponents had a lot of our film to study and were gunning for us. We were the kings of the conference and they were coming after us."

Boarding a team bus to leave for the Portland airport, Hoffmann gingerly took a seat surrounded by Clifford, Rohrbach and little brother Stevie. Despite the excruciating pain in his foot, he smiled when reflecting on the big picture. A 6-0 record, the nation's #1 ranking and a winning streak now extended to 20 games.

17

CHAPTER 18

FOLLOWING A LACKLUSTER WIN over Pacific, Washington closed out the month of October with a home game on Halloween against #15 Stanford. The legendary Bill Walsh was now coaching the Cardinal. Meanwhile, Dave Hoffmann sensed a growing awareness that his days as a Husky were drawing to a close. Just four more games, plus a bowl.

They ran out of the tunnel into rain-swept Husky Stadium for a Pac-10 showdown for first place. But for the first time all season, the Dawgs fell behind when Stanford intercepted a Mark Brunell pass, then scored when quarterback Steve Stenstrom connected with Justin Armour for a 31-yard touchdown. Napoleon Kaufman struck back with a punt return of 65 yards deep into Stanford territory, and moments later tied the score with a Leif Johnson touchdown dive.

Dave's little brother Steve Hoffmann made his first collegiate start, recording a sack and a fumble recovery. "I loved watching Steve develop as a player," Hoff says. "He was starting to come into his own and make big plays. Not just do his job, but dominate his blocker and get off the block and make plays. It helped build his confidence."

"My first start was against Stanford," recalled Steve Hoffmann. "I recovered a fumble and got mobbed by Clifford and Dave. We were all so jacked up. With the camaraderie we had, we wanted to celebrate with each other and pump each other up."

Stanford may have scored the first touchdown but it was all Washington after that. The Huskies scored 41 straight points and won 41-7. Mark Brunell was fully healed from his knee injury and scrambling and throwing at his best. Napoleon Kaufman rushed 11 times for 87 yards. And in the third quarter a heart-warming moment occurred that none of the UW players will forget.

"I was blitzing up the middle as the quarterback dropped back to pass," Hoffmann says. "I beat the blocker and hit the QB right in the chest as he threw the ball. As I was lying on top of him I could hear the roar of the crowd. I looked over and saw James Clifford rumbling down the sideline. The quarterback was trying to get up, and I just held onto him and smiled and said, 'Nope. Sorry.' I watched James and an escort of teammates run into the end zone."

"Glyn Milburn came out of the backfield and basically caught the pass, but I ripped the ball out of his hands," recalled James Clifford. "This was on the Stanford 42-yard line. I was trying so hard to run so fast that I was going nowhere. We had defensive linemen running alongside me and defensive backs back-peddling into the end zone and escorting me in. We got a personal foul because the whole defense and whole bench were celebrating. I thought Coach James was going to blow a gasket. But it turned out that he was as happy as anybody that I scored."

With an 8-0 record and the winning streak at 22 games, a third straight Rose Bowl seemed inevitable. Years later, KJR analyst Hugh Millen looked back at that moment and placed it into historical context. He said if those who follow Husky Football created a graph that charted the program's entire history going back to 1889, then October 31, 1992 would be the apex, the highest point. The team had become monolithic beyond anything it had ever known.

Little did anyone know that a different type of adversity was on the horizon.

CHAPTER 19

THURSDAY NOVEMBER 5, 1992 started like a seemingly normal day for Dave Hoffmann. "I had to go to the training room every morning for my foot to get worked on," he says. "That was mandatory. Even if I didn't have class, I couldn't sleep in. I had to get the foot taken care of and put the boot on and lug that thing around like a pirate with a wooden leg. We had a road game against Arizona that Saturday, and I wanted to be ready.

"James Clifford and I had a favorite routine of going to the Burgermaster in University Village and having breakfast. On the way back in James's Bronco, we were coming down Montlake Boulevard with the sports radio station on. Suddenly there was breaking news. They were saying that Billy Joe Hobert had received a $50,000 loan. Me and James both reached over at the same time to turn the volume up. I was thinking that it wasn't April Fool's Day but it had to be some kind of joke. We were looking at each other like, *What the hell?* We didn't even know what to say. The program was so squeaky clean it was unfathomable. Under Don James the ship ran tight and we were all on board. We had no idea how that could be going on."

UW athletic director Barbara Hedges suspended Billy Joe Hobert within 24 hours, and he never played another down for Washington. Newspaper headlines shouted the news while local sports radio shows featured agitated callers and frenetic speculation. "Very quickly this became the thing that all of Seattle was talking about," Hoffmann says. "People were coming up to us in droves wanting to know what we knew. I didn't know anything, and I didn't want to talk to anybody about it anyway. I wanted to get our minds back on Arizona. They were a great team and we would have our hands full playing at their stadium."

Practice that week was crisp and hard-hitting. Mark Brunell was now the man at quarterback, and the whole team had complete confidence in him. As the team boarded a plane bound for Arizona, Hoff was gauging the mindset of his teammates. He saw a group of players ready to get after it.

"As the game started I was in the element I loved," Hoffmann says. "Playing on grass in the sun and heat. The game was a war and defensively we got after it." As it happened, Arizona's defense was every bit as magnificent as Washington's that day. A battle of field goals played out until the final minutes of the fourth quarter.

Arizona had the ball with a 9-3 lead, as they attempted to run out the clock. Out of desperation, the Husky defense took wild risks in trying to force a turnover. But the Wildcats methodically pushed the ball down the field until they reached Washington's goal line with less than a minute left. The raucous home crowd surged forward and endlessly roared U of A!... U of A!... U of A!

"I can speak for all the guys on defense, we poured our hearts out in that game," Hoffmann says. "It was a hot day on grass. My brother Steve, Clifford, Jaime Fields, David Richie, Jamal Fountaine, Mike Ewaliko, D'Marco Farr, Shane Pahukoa, everyone gave it their all. You could see it in everyone's eyes. It was the realization that, 'hey guys, we're not going to win this one.' We hadn't lost a game in two years, not since the UCLA game in 1990. Jamal and D'Marco came over to me spontaneously as we broke huddle the last time to give me a hug and say 'I love ya Hoff.'"

"I just felt bad for Dave and James Clifford," said Jamal Fountaine. "Because Hoff and Cloff were the focal point of our defense at that time. I also just remembered the guys who had carried the torch before that: the Steve Emtmans, the Dana Halls, the Chico Fraleys, the Dennis Browns... Even on offense, guys like Mark Brunnell and

Billy Joe Hobert, and the coaches who had been doing such a phenomenal job week after week. To have lost that game at Arizona in such a fashion — it was basically a phone booth fight. When I looked over at Dave in the game's final seconds, he just epitomized the toughness of what we were. Playing hurt, and being rugged— I considered Hoff a rugged player. The nastiest, legal player out there on the football field was Dave Hoffmann. I wanted to make sure that I paid my respect to him as a player and to let him know that I looked up to him as a teammate. And I still look up to him to this day."

"It was an acknowledgement that the winning streak was coming to an end," Hoff says. "We had battled hard. Not just that day, but we had battled hard for a long time, we had battled hard for years. We had a hell of a run with that winning streak. It was an acknowledgment of all the hard work we had put in and the hunt. Just the love and respect for each other, which I had for all my teammates. I've said it many times but I played not only with the greatest players in the world, but also the greatest people. The kind of guys that even to this day I would do anything for. On a day like that, you just appreciate your teammates. We were all playing with injuries and my body was killing me. But we still fought to the end.

"I got into my stance and waited for that final snap," Hoff says. "I was dehydrated and hot, and I took a moment there and thought...I love this! I love this feeling I have right now. It's being out here engaged in the fight and it's what I love. I'm out here pouring everything I have into a great fight."

As the final seconds ticked down the Arizona fans pushed up to the edge of the bleachers. "They were going to rush the field," Hoffmann says. "I told my brother 'KEEP YOUR HELMET ON! STAY TOGETHER! WE'RE GONNA HAVE TO FIGHT OUR WAY OUTTA HERE!' Sure enough, the fans raided the field but nobody jacked with us. We got to the tunnel and locker room with no problem.

"Some speculated that we were distracted heading into that game," Dave recalls. "But I thought we had our heads in the right place. We just happened to be playing a very good team that played the best game of their lives because we were the best thing they'd seen. We had circumstances go against us, but you can't complain. Some people cited the turnovers we had in that game, but defenses create turnovers. Arizona forced some that day. Our defense needed to make something happen but we couldn't get that extra turnover. But we left it all out there on the field. I was so freaking tired and my body hurt so badly. I knew that there was nothing more I could have done physically or mentally to win that game."

James Clifford couldn't bring himself to acknowledge the outcome in the same way. "We were better than Arizona," Clifford said. "We were a better team than them. We had better talent than them. We allowed the Billy Joe Hobert situation to infiltrate our team and distract us from the task at hand. I really feel that to be the truth. We allowed something beyond our control to affect us. We were all young men. We were affected by the uncertainty of not knowing what was going to happen to our football team... I felt responsible. It was pretty sad, after all the work we had put in, that things took that kind of turn."

On the flight back to Seattle, a dehydrated Dave Hoffmann sat back in his seat fighting through a surge of emotions. He arrived home very late that night and endured a fitful sleep. "I was nauseous and spent the night dry heaving," he says. "When I woke up the next morning and went to the bathroom mirror, my reflection scared the hell out of me. My eyes were pure red. I called my mom, who was a nurse, and she said I would be fine, and that I'd broken all my capillaries. When I went to the trainers for my foot, they confirmed that my eyes would be fine.

"It had been an emotional week," Hoff reflected. "We had been so close my sophomore year in 1990 to winning the national championship. We won the whole thing in 1991. Then we thought we had a good shot at winning it all again in 1992. But offensively, some things didn't go our way. Some dropped passes and turnovers hurt us. This is not to take anything away from Arizona as they were a very good team—aggressive and physical.

"We had been the target, with the bull's eye on our chest for a long time. We got the best game Arizona ever played. I still had to give thanks to God for being able to run around and battle out there with my teammates. I was thankful for that Saturday."

As a result of the Arizona loss, the Huskies tumbled in the national rankings. But one more win would clinch a third straight trip to the Rose Bowl. A home game against Oregon State was next on the schedule—and Hoffmann's last as a Husky. "I made a note in my head to let myself enjoy and soak in my final time playing in Husky Stadium. The things that made the University of Washington special were the people: the fans, teammates, coaches and staff. I felt very thankful. I go on and on about my teammates, but the bottom line is that I love them. No matter what we've all been through, nobody's perfect. When asked about Billy Joe, our answer is we don't hold grudges. God forgives us and we all forgive each other and don't hold grudges on anything. It's easy to get along and have fun with guys like that. We'd all been through a lot. We had had an unbelievable run in Seattle."

The next Saturday, Washington trounced Oregon State 45-16 to capture their third straight Pac-10 title and Rose Bowl berth. Afterwards the stadium quickly emptied out, but Hoff and the other seniors lingered. They looked around, grasping to comprehend the passage of time and realizing that never again would they play football in Husky Stadium. "I was shaking hands with guys from Oregon State and looked over and saw Lambright and boy did that make my heart smile," Hoffmann says. "He had come down early. He was usually up in the press box making calls and would meet us in the team room. We got a picture taken of me, Lambright and James Clifford, and that meant a lot.

"I had flashbacks to being a homesick freshman and compared it to where I was at now. It's hard to say for sure, but I thought I exceeded my expectations I had set for myself. I came up from San

Jose as kind of an undersized guy who could hit. I tried to squeeze every ounce of ability from myself. It was an honor to play someplace that historically had so many great linebackers. I was really honored to have filled that spot for a few years. I hoped that I had made all the old linebackers proud as well as my parents.

"I lingered awhile longer with my brother and all the guys on defense. I gave Mark Brunell a hug and all the other seniors that I came in with. We didn't need to say much, just give each other hug and a nod. We knew what we had been through. We walked off the field with each of us holding a rose."

For the third year in a row, a representative from the Rose Bowl addressed the team and officially extended the offer to play in Pasadena. "Three in a row," Hoffmann said. "We knew it was an accomplishment. Nobody in the locker room took it for granted because we knew how much work went into it. You wonder if people who show up on Saturday had any idea how much pain and work went into getting to that point. You wondered if people began taking it for granted."

There was still one game left for the 9-1 Huskies —on the road at Washington State. This game ended up going down in Cougar folklore as the "Snow Bowl". A blizzard engulfed the small college town of Pullman and Martin Stadium. From his hotel room that morning, Hoffmann peered through the window and thought to himself, *Let it snow, brother!* "Beforehand I was fired up and thinking it was going to be like one of those epic NFL games you've seen played at Soldier Field or Lambeau Field on the so-called frozen tundra," Hoffmann says. "Actually, I had no idea what the footing was going to be like once we got out there. It also came as a surprise that the Cougars barely plowed the field. It was actually a smart move, as the Cougars could put on longer cleats and we were stuck with our low profile turf shoes. We found out during warm-ups that we could barely stand up out there.

"You know, football is one of those things where you don't take much time to worry; you go with what you have," Hoffmann says.

"You have to find a way to make it happen. We went out there with that intent, but man oh man, we had a rough time. Our defensive linemen couldn't push to take that initial step and fire off the ball. To get that inertia that you would normally get in normal conditions.

"The Cougs did some smart things with their pass routes. They ran routes where receivers didn't make multiple cuts and that proved effective because our guys were at a severe disadvantage just from trying to move and get out of a two point stance. If I was covering the tight end, I would get my hands on him and not let him get away from me. That's what I decided to do and if the refs threw a flag then they threw a flag—but they never did. They probably couldn't see me through all the snow and sleet coming down."

Washington State's Drew Bledsoe had an epic day throwing the football, as the Cougars routed the Huskies 42-23. In a play that's been replayed countless times throughout the Pacific Northwest, Cougar wide receiver Philip Bobo catches a Bledsoe pass in the back of the end zone and slides several feet across the slick and icy turf. "That pass was actually intended for C.J. Davis," recalled Bobo. "Drew threw that ball up for C.J. and I just saw it and decided that I was going to make the catch. Fox Sports has shown it in several commercials and when the Apple Cup rolls around every year it gets replayed. Fans still bring it up to me all the time."

The regular season had come to an end. Washington was 9-2 and headed to the Rose Bowl for a rematch against the undefeated Big 10 champion Michigan Wolverines. "It was unfortunate to lose two games so quickly," Hoffmann says. "It didn't feel right. But I was looking forward to playing in the warm weather against a great Michigan team again."

CHAPTER 20

DAVE HOFFMANN SAVORED EVERY moment of Thanksgiving. He had several days for his body to heal up from the abuses of the regular season, before beginning preparations for Michigan. The announcement came that he had won the Pac-10 Defensive Player of the Year award. Teammate Lincoln Kennedy won the Morris Trophy as the league's best lineman.

Nationally, Hoff was named as one of three finalists for the Butkus Award, honoring college football's best linebacker. The award is named for Dick Butkus, the ferocious All-American at Illinois who became a NFL Hall-of-Famer with the Chicago Bears. The reputation of Butkus knew no bounds. Back in the mid-1960s, when he was going to play against the Green Bay Packers for the first time, legendary coach Vince Lombardi growled "Let's smear this kid's face." However, Butkus manhandled blockers and devastated ball carriers. After the game, Lombardi said: "He's the best who ever played the position."

"Being a finalist was an honor not just for me but for the entire Husky defense," Hoffmann says. "When they told me they were going to fly me and my parents out there to Orlando I thought that was a neat deal. That first night there was a blast. Eating shrimp and having a drink and talking with the great Dick Butkus. As you would expect, he couldn't have been more humble and gracious. He was great to my mom and dad. The next day I played golf with my dad. Keith Jackson from ABC-TV was in the group in front of us and

Butkus was in the group behind us.

"The night of the event, we were all decked out in tuxes," Hoff says. "There was a big crowd and large banners hanging all around. This was the first black tie event I had been to in my life. The finalists were myself, Marvin Jones of Florida State and Michael Barrows of Miami. Keith Jackson introduced us to the crowd. When it was my turn at the podium, I gave thanks that I was there and that I was blessed to play linebacker. I recognized my defense that had been so dominant up in Seattle. After we all had a chance to speak, we waited for the announcement to be made. Marvin and Michael were great guys and we got along well. They showed a lot of respect for our defense, which meant a lot. It's nice when the media recognizes your success, but its best when your colleagues do so."

Marvin Jones was announced the winner, and he returned to the podium as applause sounded throughout the room. Hoffmann stood behind him on the stage listening.

Suddenly, someone whispered... *"Psst! Hey Hoffmann!*

"I realized it was Butkus," Hoff says. "He was standing about six feet away from me. But the cameras were rolling and the speech was underway. I didn't want to do anything to take away from Marvin's moment. But again, I hear from Butkus... *'Hey Hoffmann! Hey Dave!'*

"I thought I better look over," Hoff says. "Butkus said to me, *'We've got a bunch of beer up in my suite. When this thing's over, come up to my room and we'll have a beer!'*

"I wanted to say 'Yes sir,' but I thought it would seem too formal. So I nodded and whispered, 'You bet.'"

After the ceremony concluded, Hoffmann went back to his room and changed out of his tuxedo and into a casual shirt and jeans. He went up to the suite and knocked. The door swung open and Butkus was there along with friends and members of the Butkus family. Bow ties were loosened and dress shirts were un-tucked. "COME ON IN!", Butkus bellowed.

Dave entered the cavernous suite and accepted a cold beer. He took a seat upon one of the ritzy couches flanking a large coffee table.

He and Butkus began talking. It turned out that not only was Butkus a NFL Hall-of-Fame linebacker, he had also played for the Illinois team that beat Washington and a young Jim Lambright in the 1964 Rose Bowl.

"I had already been around him for a couple days and had gotten to know him a bit," Hoffmann says. "He was just a great guy and really down to earth. We talked football and family. Being younger than the others there, I tended to keep quiet and do more listening than talking. That whole thing was a real treat for me. You work hard for a long time and when little moments like that come around you really appreciate them."

Dave Hoffmann's last day as a Husky came on January 1, 1993 at Pasadena's Rose Bowl. Each moment was to be savored. Awakening at the hotel with that feeling of anticipation in the gut. Sitting one last time on the team bus to the stadium with brother Steve, James Clifford and Mike Rohrbach. Getting taped up by trainers before heading out to the immaculate field for stretching and drills.

"There's a photo taken in pre-game warm ups from that Rose Bowl," said Mike Rohrbach. "It's a picture of Dave with blood dripping down his nose. It's just the intensity of Hoff. I have it at home in my den. He signed it *Dear Rohr, Laying the Hammer for Jesus. Love, Hoff.*"

The game got underway and the rematch quickly proved a shootout. Michigan's Tyrone Wheatley set a Rose Bowl record when he raced up the middle untouched for an 88-yard touchdown. "We went out there and gave it our all," Hoff says. "The frustrating thing was Michigan's trap play. We struggled in adjusting to it. They had watched our films all December and prepared that play for us."

Mark Brunell, in his last game as a Husky, had a spectacular day, throwing for 308 yards. On one play, he threw deep down the center of the field and freshman receiver Jason Shelley caught it over a defender for the 64-yard touchdown reception.

At the end of the third quarter the game was knotted at 31-31. But Michigan scored in the fourth quarter and won 38-31. Washington's bid to make history with three straight Rose Bowl titles fell short. Michigan quarterback Elvis Grbac ran over to the cheering Michigan fans with his arms raised in triumph.

"We had a mutual respect with the Michigan linemen and congratulated them after the game," Hoffmann says. "A mournful feeling entered my heart in knowing my career at Washington was over. When you pour so much into it something it's an emotional moment to see it end. Seeing my brother come up to me on the field and give me a hug was a moment I'll never forget. We didn't have to say much. We knew how blessed we were to have played together for such a great defense and teammates. Our eyes were watery. It was hard not to cry. My brother and I walked slowly off the field together, just like the countless times we walked slowly down the tunnel to practice at Husky Stadium. I took my time in the Rose Bowl locker room. I walked around and gave guys farewell hugs. I saw Lambright and walked toward him."

"Dave and I hugged and there was nothing to say other than expressing appreciation," Jim Lambright recalled. "The fact we lost the game was almost an unnecessary exclamation point that didn't have anything to do with the memories. I remember the tears and extreme emotions from the loss. At the same time, it was such a great group of players, and it felt surreal. I said, 'This loss does nothing to take away from everything that has been accomplished.' In my mind, in spite of tears and in spite of the results themselves, it was still the end to the great careers of some super people, to the great number of wins that we had... It was the best thing that has ever happened to me."

That night was quiet for Hoffmann. He had dinner with his family and then went back to the hotel and socialized a bit with teammates. "But that was it," he says. "That was it, man.

"I had learned a lot. I had gotten the most out of my years at Washington. No regrets. I made mistakes but I learned valuable lessons to take me forward. I learned what it took to be a man both spiritually and socially. I knew it was an ongoing process. I learned that the guys that think they have it all figured out are the ones you worry about. I had come to realize how much I needed God. I needed all the forgiveness and help I could get. I learned that giving full effort and having a great attitude would always be incredibly important. I was really tested. The Bible says to lean on Him. I realized that it wasn't like putting an arm on a buddy and relaxing. It meant to lean on Him like you would lean on a wall. As if the wall moved you would fall over. That's because He will never fail you. That's what I learned to do at Washington."

17

EPILOGUE

IN AUGUST 1993, DAVE Hoffmann was a rookie linebacker for the Chicago Bears when he got the call from his brother Steve in Seattle. "He said that the Pac-10 had just concluded their investigation of the football program and had given them severe sanctions. He said that Don James had just stepped down as coach in protest. Steve was furious. He had broken the big plate window by the training room by punching it. Everybody back in Seattle was just furious. Steve was becoming a leader on that team. My words to him were: *Keep the oven door closed. Don't let that anger leave too quickly.* It's common for guys to get fired up about something and deplete that energy. Whether it was something good or bad I liked to use things like that as energy to fuel my fire.

"Those guys were angered and saddened by a lot of things," recalls Hoff. "As everybody knows, those brutal sanctions were a disgrace. Billy Joe Hobert's loan was received from a family friend with no ties to the football program. The thing the league cited were discrepancies in the summer jobs program in Southern California. From my vantage point in Chicago, the Pac-10's hind ends were sore from the last few years of being whipped by Washington. Instead of making a professional decision based on whatever minor violations they found in their investigation, they took another approach. In my opinion their jealously got the best of them.

"It was a cowardly thing. If those other teams wanted to be the Pac-10 champion they should have recruited harder, worked harder and tried to earn it. Don't just penalize Washington. It made me sick for the Husky players. Don James ran a squeaky clean program with a bunch of great players and guys."

The Pac-10 rendered Washington ineligible to play in bowl games for '93 and '94, and also cut 20 available scholarships. But they kept the popular Huskies on TV. "The big one was they weren't going to give us TV revenue (about $2.8 million)," said Don James in the book *Husky Football in the Don James Era*. "They wanted our money. We'd made this league so damn much money. They didn't want to take us off TV. They wanted that money."

Under new coach Jim Lambright, the Huskies only won a combined 14 games the next two years. There were notable wins, including the "Whammy in Miami" in 1994 down at the Orange Bowl, where the Huskies beat the Hurricanes 38-20 to snap Miami's NCAA record 58-game home winning streak.

"One thing I realized is that you don't understand how good of a teammate you have until they're gone," said Steve Hoffmann. "I've tried to remember that in my life with relatives, friends, teammates and family members. To make note of them and appreciate them while they're here. Because when they're gone, nothing can quite fill that void. Talk about a leader. Talk about a guy that everyone wants to be around. Dave makes friends instantly. I appreciate that about him. Guys want to be around him. He leads by example. You want that kind of guy on your team.

"After Dave left for the NFL, a lot of guys picked where he left off with some stuff that he did. During drills he always encouraged guys but also got after them if they weren't giving their all. The remaining guys started to pick that up, but you can't replicate it. That only comes from a born leader. Those other guys would do it differently, and nobody could do it exactly the way Dave did. Both he and Emtman were twins in that regard. They would lead by example and get after guys. It wasn't quite the same after they were gone."

Dave Hoffmann's NFL career ended entering his third year in 1995. His body was breaking down and hindered by certain injuries that were slow to heal. He got married and his wife Elle gave birth to two children. The Hoffmanns lived on the east coast and remained there for many years. All the while he longed for Husky Stadium and missed the gameday experience. He tried catching games on east coast TV when he could, and watched with dismay as the powerhouse program he once played for steadily unraveled under coaches Keith Gilbertson (2003-2004) and Tyrone Willingham (2005-2008). Under Willingham, the Huskies became the first Pac-10 team to ever go 0-12; a mere 17 years after the Dawgs went undefeated.

On a July evening in 2009, Dave sat back to relax and flip channels at the end of a long day. He was watching *The Late Show with David Letterman*, and got a kick out of seeing actor Joel McHale being interviewed. McHale, the star of NBC's hit show *Community*, once played on UW's scout team and earned a Rose Bowl ring back in the early 90s. Dave broke out into a big smile at seeing McHale's career going so well.

McHale began telling a story from the old days. He disclosed how he lied to UW coaches in order to get on the team. Then he described what it was like being a tight end and running a crossing route in practice against the first team defense.

"We ran a play," McHale said. "And this guy named Dave Hoffmann, he was an All-American and he's a monster, and he knocked the wind out of me so hard that my lung looked like a bubble coming out of my mouth."

Letterman and the audience laughed. McHale said that the UW coaches liked the play so much they ordered the scout team to run it again. So the scrubs put it into motion, and once again Hoffmann blasted McHale nearly unconscious.

McHale described seeing stars and struggling to get to his feet, only to hear the coaches order them to run it a third time. Woozy, he lined up and glanced over at Hoffmann. "He was smiling," McHale said. "And he said *You're okay this time*. And they said 'HIKE!' and I ran right off the field... The only time I ever got the respect of my teammates was during skit night."

In November 2011, members of the 1991 National Championship team gathered in Seattle for a 20th year reunion. The same weekend the current-day Huskies hosted the powerhouse Oregon Ducks. It was also a farewell to Husky Stadium, which was about to undergo a massive renovation.

Hoffmann arrived in Seattle that Thursday. Teammates were flying in from all over the country. "We had waited for the reunion for so long," Hoff recalls. "On the Friday before the game I was on campus in Red Square about to go on the air with KJR Radio. I had to establish a cut off time with them because they were running late. They said 'WHAT? YOU'VE GOT TO LEAVE?' I said, 'Yes I do. I've got to pick up James Clifford at the airport. I'm not going to be late for that!' Cliffy was flying in from his home in Arizona. My brother and I drove to Sea-Tac Airport and seeing him again fired me up."

"Dave picked me up at the airport and we went to see a bunch of the guys," recalled Clifford. "It felt like my recruiting trip and meeting Dave for the first time. It felt like, HEY, EVERYBODY'S HERE! Dave was the best man in my wedding. We've known each other for more than twenty years. We're probably closer today than we were back then."

On Friday night, the horde of former players took over tables at a popular restaurant called The Ram. "We sat around and talked for over five hours," Hoffmann says.

"Later on, while continuing the celebration at the Crew House, the linebackers gathered for a group photo beneath a picture of the late Jaime Fields. Then we moved over to the newly renovated Crew House. We couldn't believe the old shack looked so good. Coach James and the '91 captains spoke to the team."

"Coach James spoke to all of us at the Crew House," said former linebacker Jamal Fountaine. "All eyes were on him. It was the same words. He used to address us as men, and he addressed in the same way again. Coach Lambright was there. Seeing Hoff and Cloff, Steve Emtman, Chico Fraley, Hillary Butler, Donald Jones, Darius Turner and all those guys was great. Unfortunately, D'Marco Farr and Ed Cunningham had to work (as football broadcasters) and couldn't be there. But almost all the guys and all the components were there. I fell right back into the rank and file. The faces were exactly the same and the attitudes were exactly the same. We were all just a little bit heavier."

"I hope more Husky teams have the opportunity to have reunions like we did," Hoffmann says. "We don't have to find reasons to get together; we just need to get together! Sitting there yapping with the guys, I found out about their families and what they're up to these days. Some guys are still in great shape, others have paunches, thinning hair or glasses. We laughed so hard and cried about the old days and about how much fun we had. Those days really did make us who we are. From our parents raising us up and then going to play in that era with those coaches and teammates. I thank the Lord to this day that I played and battled with that special group of warriors."

The weekend held deep meaning for former linebacker Donald Jones, who flew in from his home in North Carolina. "Twenty years had passed but it was like no time had passed," Jones said. "We didn't miss a beat. We picked up where we left off. I saw Dave and gave him a big hug. It was only the second time I had seen him in person since we played. We have kept in contact through the years through email and Facebook. But to see him again, that's greatness. Not just as a football player but as a person. Going through what we did together, and accomplishing what we did, we made history. Our kids and grandkids will be able to read about what we did. And someone like Dave is someone that you call a friend and that you love. That's the thing about Dave, he's one of those cats that will tell you that he loves you. Not too many men will say that. But man, that's how our relationship is."

"It was a very emotional weekend for me," recalled former linebacker Chico Fraley. "A lot of the guys I hadn't seen in fifteen or twenty years. It struck me how easily old relationships were rekindled.

I have had the fortune of seeing Dave and Cliff more recently than some of the other guys. But having the ability to see that everyone is now raising kids and that has become the joy of our lives now. To see the old guys and cherish all the work that we did together. The things we talked about the most weren't the games, but the little drills we did and the competitions we had in practice. And the genuine care we had for each other."

"It was also really great to see Billy Joe Hobert there," said Jamal Fountaine. "I hadn't talked to Billy since all the stuff went down twenty years ago. I had seen him when we were in the NFL but I never had a chance to really talk with him. For him to come back, and everybody hug him up like we did, I'm sure had to feel good to him. And it felt great to me. Because we wouldn't have accomplished any of that without him. I don't care what nobody says. Billy Joe never lost a high school game and never lost a college game (that he played in), so there you go."

The following night at Husky Stadium featured more beautiful moments, just not on the field. The modern day Huskies were no match for the Ducks, who would go on to win their first Rose Bowl since 1917. But at the end of the third quarter, the 1991 National Championship team assembled along the sideline and prepared to step into the end zone for the introduction. The players jabbered amongst themselves, with Hoffmann loudly suggesting to Shane Pahukoa that the entire team walk all the way to midfield. The players hooted and hollered approval.

The PA announcer boomed: PLEASE DIRECT YOUR ATTENTION TO THE WEST END ZONE..." The team received their cue and stepped forward en masse, to thunderous applause from the Husky Stadium crowd. "I started walking out there toward midfield and upon reaching the 10-yard line sensed something was up," Hoffmann says. "I turned around, and everyone else had stopped at the 2-yard line!"

Soon after, Dave Hoffmann was back home in Southern California. He was seated at the dinner table looking at his wife and kids.

He realized the apple didn't fall far from the tree. His 11-year old son Jaeger will be playing football for the first time in the fall of 2012.

"He's starting out a bit earlier than I did," Hoff says. "He's fired up about it and has wanted to play for years. From an early age he's always loved to wrestle with me and he's very physical. I'll be happy with however far he goes, but it will be fun to watch him have fun out there. I'll be proud of him no matter what, he's a great young man.

"Just this morning I was watching my 14-year old daughter Callie out on the soccer field," Hoffmann says. "You couldn't help but notice she was by far the most physical person in the game. All within the rules. They had to stop the game a few times so coaches could go out and tend to players lying horizontal on the ground, and make sure they were okay.

"I sit back and don't say much during her games. But this morning I was coming down the bleacher steps and a couple of parents said 'I wish they all played a bit more like Callie.' I smiled and said, 'I'm glad that she can let it out and have fun out there. That's the thing about sports. When you're out there on the field, you can let it all hang out and be yourself. But when you step back over the sideline and return to society, you've got to toe the line and act all civil. But out there you can be yourself.'

"The parents looked at me like I was nuts," Hoffmann recalls.

"But it's great that Callie understands that," he says. "I don't have to say anything. She just goes out there and brings it every time." Hoff was asked if that type of aggression was in the genes or was learned. "It's a question that I couldn't have answered until I had kids of my own," Hoff replied. "I do think it's both. At a very young age, I would see a look in my kids' eyes as they grit their teeth, and I would recoil and think 'Holy cow! They're Mini-Me's!' I haven't even had time to ruin them yet.

"I never showed Callie how to use her body to devastate her opponents in a proper, legal way. She just goes out there and does it. Man, those others kids didn't want to come down the middle of the field. She was stalking prey. Just like Jaeger, she's got the physical tools like size and speed. But she also has the innate intensity and passion for the game… and passion for the hunt. I do think some of that's in the genes. There's some DNA at work there."

Something else was at work and revealed itself later that spring of 2012. Hoff was visiting his brother Matt at his home in Chicago. As various family members hung out in the living room, jabbering and joking, Dave's cell phone suddenly rang. He answered it and heard his wife's voice calling from California.

"Honey," she said. "Don James called, he's looking for you. Please call him right away."

Dave sat upright. His former coach was now almost 80. "Is everything alright?" he asked.

"Everything's fine," she said. "Just call him right away. *Please* don't wait."

Hoff agreed and terminated the call. Matt gave him a puzzled look.

"Not sure what's going on," Hoff said. "Don James called looking for me."

"Might be serious," Matt said.

"I'm gonna call him back from the kitchen," replied Hoff.

Dave went by himself into the next room and stood near a window. He dialed the number and gazed into the yard while holding the phone to his ear.

"Coach James — it's Dave Hoffmann."

"Hi Dave."

The two men spent time inquiring about each other's families and shared a couple quips. Finally, Coach James got to the point.

"Dave, I've got good news for you."

"Oh, yeah?"

"This October, you're being inducted into the Husky Hall of Fame," he said.